John Farmer

Hymns and Chorales

John Farmer

Hymns and Chorales

ISBN/EAN: 9783744774512

Printed in Europe, USA, Canada, Australia, Japan

Cover: Foto ©Paul-Georg Meister /pixelio.de

More available books at **www.hansebooks.com**

HYMNS AND CHORALES

JOHN FARMER

London

HENRY FROWDE

OXFORD UNIVERSITY PRESS WAREHOUSE
AMEN CORNER, E.C.

New York

MACMILLAN AND CO.
112 FOURTH AVENUE

Hymns and Chorales

for

Schools and Colleges

EDITED BY

JOHN FARMER

ORGANIST OF BALLIOL COLLEGE

Oxford
AT THE CLARENDON PRESS
1892

Oxford
PRINTED AT THE CLARENDON PRESS
BY HORACE HART, PRINTER TO THE UNIVERSITY

PREFACE

THE purpose of this Book is to give a short selection of the best Hymns and Chorales suitable for Schools and Colleges.

The selection is chiefly made from lists of Hymns sent me by some whom I thought best qualified to judge, in answer to the question, 'What Hymns are the best and most suitable for Schools and Colleges?'

I am indebted to the following for their kind aid in this matter:—

The Right Rev. the Lord Bishop of Durham.
The Rev. the Master of Trinity College, Cambridge.
The Rev. the Master of Balliol College, Oxford.
The Principal of Brasenose College, Oxford.
The Rev. the Rector of Lincoln College, Oxford.
The Rev. the Head Master of Harrow School.
H. R. Reichel, Esq., Principal of University College, Bangor.
Walter Leaf, Esq., Trinity College, Cambridge.
The late R. L. Nettleship, Esq., Balliol College, Oxford.

As to the Tunes, I have endeavoured to select only the very best.

I have to thank the following gentlemen for kindly allowing me to use copyright Hymns:

The Rev. J. Ellerton, the Rev. Canon Furse, the Rev. Father Neville, the Rev. F. Pott, the Rev. H. Twells, the Rev. N. R. Toke, Otto Goldschmidt, Esq., the Committee of *Hymns Ancient and Modern*, Messrs. Longmans, Green & Co., George Bell & Sons, James Nisbet & Co., J. Masters & Co., and the Religious Tract Society.

Every effort has been made to discover the owners of Copyright, but should the copyright of any hymn have been unintentionally infringed, it is hoped that the error will be pardoned.

My special thanks are due to E. J. Palmer, Esq., Fellow of Balliol College, for his translations from the German, and to E. Walker, Esq., Balliol College, for most valuable help.

My excuse for attempting this selection is my long connection with Public School Life and the encouragement of the Master of Balliol College.

J. F.

Oxford, 1892.

SHORT BIOGRAPHIES OF ENGLISH HYMN-WRITERS

ADDISON, Joseph (1672-1719), a celebrated English author, best known as a writer of Essays, which appeared in the *Tatler*, *Spectator*, and *Guardian*, and from the time of their first publication have maintained their rank as English Classics. He was the son of Lancelot Addison, Dean of Lichfield, and was educated first at Charterhouse School, and then at Queen's College, Oxford, whence he migrated to Magdalen College, of which he became a Fellow. A walk in the College grounds still retains his name. Besides being a prose writer he was also a poet, the author of the once famous, now forgotten, tragedy of Cato, and of several other pieces, Latin as well as English. He was also for a short time Secretary of State. He died at Holland House, then in the possession of his wife, the Countess of Warwick, 1719.

ANSTICE, Joseph (1808-1836), the son of William Anstice, of Madeley, Salop, was educated at Enmore, near Bridgewater, Westminster, and Christ Church, Oxford, where he gained two English prizes and graduated as a double-first. Subsequently, at the age of 22, he became Professor of Classical Literature at King's College, London. He died at Torquay, February 29, 1836, aged 28. His hymns were printed a few months after his death.

AUBER, Harriet (1773-1862), was born in London, and lived during her long life principally at Hoddesdon. She was the author of the *Spirit of the Psalms*, a metrical version of the *Psalter* (1829), and of several other poetical works.

AUSTIN, John (1613-1669), was born at Walpole in Norfolk. He was educated at Sleaford Grammar School and at St. John's College, Cambridge. He became a Roman Catholic in 1640, and, quitting the University, went to London, where he entered at Lincoln's Inn. He died in 1669. The work by which he is chiefly known is a volume of *Devotions*, containing 'Psalms, Hymns, and Prayers, for every Day in the Week and every Holiday in the Year,' which was published at Rouen after his death.

BAKER, Sir Henry Williams (1821-1877), was born in London, and educated at Trinity College, Cambridge. In 1851 he was made Vicar of Monkland, near Leominster, where he remained until his death. He was the editor of the well-known collection *Hymns Ancient and Modern*, to which he himself made several contributions.

BAXTER, Richard (1615-1691), was born at Rowton in Shropshire. His early education was desultory and imperfect, but he was afterwards sent for three years to a school at Wroxeter, and lastly to a Mr. Wickstead, Chaplain to the Council at Ludlow Castle. His tutor persuaded him to go up to Court, but a month at Whitehall sufficed to disgust him with a courtier's life. He returned to the country, took orders in 1638, and in 1641 became assistant minister at Kidderminster. During the Civil War he spent some time with the army under Cromwell, but finally returned to Kidderminster, where he remained until 1660. He took an active part in the Restoration, and was offered the Bishopric of Hereford, which he declined. In 1662, on the passing of the Act of Uniformity, he left the Church of England. He died in 1691, in the seventy-sixth year of his age. The life of Baxter is an epitome of the troubled times in which his lot was cast. Though weak and sickly in constitution, he was indefatigable both as a preacher and writer. Of his numerous works the best remembered and most widely known is *The Saint's Everlasting Rest*.

BONAR, Horatio (1808-1889), a native of Edinburgh, was minister at Kelso from 1837 to 1867, and afterwards of a church in Edinburgh. He was the author of several hymns which have attained a wide popularity.

BROWNE, Simon (1680-1732), was born at Shepton Mallet, and educated at local Dissenting Academies. He was first minister at Portsmouth, but became in 1716 pastor of a congregation in the Old Jewry, London. He died at Shepton Mallet in 1732. He wrote, besides various educational and controversial works, a volume of *Hymns and Spiritual Songs*.

BUCKOLL, Henry James (1803-1871), was born at Siddington, Gloucester, and educated at Rugby and Queen's College, Oxford, graduating in 1826. He became Assistant Master at Rugby in the same year, and in 1827 he took Holy Orders. He was probably the editor of the first edition of the *Rugby School Collection*, in which several of his hymns are to be found. He died at Rugby.

BURNS, Robert (1759-1796), the most celebrated of Scottish poets, was born not far from Ayr, in a cottage which his father had built with his own hands. He received some education from a village teacher, but the greater part of his knowledge was self-acquired. His life was a constant struggle against misfortune and against himself: in his own words, 'he had little art in making money and still less in keeping it.' He died at Dumfries, when only in his thirty-seventh year.

BYROM, John (1692-1763), was born at Broughton, near Manchester. He was educated at The Merchant Taylors' School and at Trinity College, Cambridge, becoming Fellow of the College in 1714. He also studied medicine at Montpellier for two years. In 1718 he began to teach in London a system of shorthand which he had invented, and had among his pupils many of the most celebrated men of his time. In 1729 he made the acquaintance of William Law, author of the *Serious Call*, by whom he, like many others, was deeply influenced. He afterwards returned to Manchester, where he died in 1763. His works include poems of a miscellaneous character and some hymns.

CENNICK, John (1718-1755), born at Reading, was descended from a family of Quakers, but was brought up in the Church of England. He assisted Wesley and Whitefield in their labours for a time, and then passed over to and became a minister of the Moravian Church. He died in London.

COSIN, John (1594-1672), was born at Norwich. He was educated at the Grammar School and at Caius College, Cambridge, of which he afterwards became Fellow. In 1634 he was elected to the Mastership of Peterhouse, and in 1640 appointed Dean of Peterborough. He soon incurred the hostility of the Parliament, and was deprived of his preferments. He then withdrew to Paris, and acted as Chaplain to Queen Henrietta Maria. Returning to England at the Restoration, he was appointed in 1660 to the Bishopric of Durham. He took a conspicuous part in the Revision of the Prayer Book in 1661. In the administration of his diocese he showed great energy and munificence. He died in London at the beginning of 1672. He was the author of some controversial treatises and of a volume of *Devotions*.

COTTON, George Edward Lynch (1813-1866), was educated at Westminster School and at Trinity College, Cambridge. In 1837 he was appointed by Dr. Arnold to a Mastership at Rugby School, and in 1852 became Head-Master of Marlborough College. He was greatly beloved by his friends and pupils. In 1858 he was made Bishop of Calcutta. He met his death by drowning in the Ganges on October 6, 1866.

COWPER, William (1731-1800), was born at Great Berkhampstead, and received his education at Westminster School. His life was overshadowed by melancholy, which led to frequent outbursts of insanity. He settled at Olney, in Bedfordshire, under the care of his friends the Unwins. Here he made the acquaintance of the curate of the parish, the Reverend John Newton, who afterwards exercised great influence over him. His poems were composed in the intervals of his malady. The *Olney Hymns*, first published in 1779, to which all collectors have been so greatly indebted, were written partly by him and partly by Newton.

CROSSMAN, Samuel (1624?-1684), was born at Monk's Bradfield in Suffolk. He graduated at Pembroke College, Cambridge, and afterwards held a living in Essex, from which he was ejected in 1662. He soon conformed again to the Establishment, and was appointed first Prebendary and then Dean of Bristol, where he died February 4, 1684. He was the author of a small devotional treatise and of a few sacred poems.

DENNY, Sir Edward, Bart., son of Sir E. Denny, fourth baronet, of Tralee Castle, County of Kerry, was born October 2, 1796, and succeeded his father in 1831. He was a member of the Plymouth Brethren, and contributed largely to their hymnody. He died in 1889.

DOANE, George Washington (1799-1859),

was born at Trenton, New Jersey, U.S., and graduated at Union College, Schenectady, New York. Ordained in 1821, he became assistant minister at Trinity Church, and in 1832 was made Bishop of New Jersey. Bishop Doane's exceptional talents, learning, and force of character, made him one of the great prelates of his time.

DODDRIDGE, Philip (1702-1751), was born in London. After receiving his education at small country schools he entered the Ministry, and in 1723 became the master of a Dissenting Academy at Northampton. Here he laboured with great energy and success until 1751, when his health failed. He then went on a voyage to Lisbon, but died there immediately after his arrival. Besides many theological works, he wrote a large number of hymns, first published in a collected form after his death.

ELLERTON, John, was born in London, December 16, 1826, and educated at Trinity College, Cambridge. He took Holy Orders, and became Rector of Barnes, 1876, and of White Roding, 1886. Mr. Ellerton's prose writings include *The Holiest Manhood*, *Our Infirmities*, &c. It is, however, as a hymnologist, editor, hymn-writer, and translator, that he is most widely known.

ELLIOTT, Charlotte (1789-1871), a popular hymn-writer, who was gifted with considerable literary talent and in her youth wrote humorous verse. After a severe illness, in 1821, she became a permanent invalid, and the influence of Cæsar Malan of Geneva, whose acquaintance she made in 1822, induced her to give up all secular pursuits. She wrote numerous religious poems, which appeared as *Hymns for a Week*, *Hours of Sorrow*; also an *Invalid's Hymn Book*, which contained 'Just as I am.' She died at Brighton.

GASCOIGNE, George (1525?-1577), a descendant of the famous judge, Sir William Gascoigne, was educated at Trinity College, Cambridge, but did not take a degree. He studied for the law in London at the Middle Temple and Gray's Inn, and afterwards spent a considerable time abroad. The remainder of his life was passed in literary pursuits. He was the author of several humorous and satirical works, as well as other poems, and has been regarded as one of the pioneers of Elizabethan literature. He died at the house of a friend, at Barnack, near Stamford, in 1577.

GIBBONS, Thomas (1720-1785), was born at Reak, Swaffham Prior, near Cambridge. He was educated at local schools and at Dissenting academies in London. He was minister to several congregations, and also tutor in the Mile End Academy. He died at Hoxton, February 22, 1785. His works, which are chiefly of a religious character, include some sacred poems and hymns.

GRANT, Sir Robert (1779-1838), was born in Bengal, and educated at Magdalen College, Cambridge. He entered at the Bar and also sat in Parliament. In 1834 he was made Governor of Bombay, where he died four years later. His hymns were first published in a collected form after his death.

GREG, Samuel (1804-1876), was the fourth son of Samuel Greg, a mill-owner at Quarry Bank, Cheshire, and brother of Robert Hyde and William Rathbone Greg. He was born at Manchester, Sept. 6, 1804, and was educated at Unitarian schools at Nottingham and Bristol. After spending some time in learning mill-work, he took, in 1832, the Lower House Mill, Bollington, and for about fifteen years the mill and the work-people were his all-absorbing objects of consideration. In 1847 he was obliged to leave the business on account of various troubles, and retired a comparatively poor man. In 1857 he began some Sunday lectures to working people, and these he continued for the remainder of his life. After a long illness he died at Bollington, May 14, 1876. At one time of his life he and his brother, William Rathbone Greg, studied and practised mesmerism with great enthusiasm. Amongst Greg's works are, *Scenes from the Life of Jesus*, and *Letters on Religious Belief*.

GURNEY, John Hampden (1802-1862), was born in London. He graduated at Trinity College, Cambridge, and afterwards became curate of Lutterworth, where he remained seventeen years. From 1842 till his death he was Rector of St. Mary's, Marylebone.

HAWEIS, Thomas (1732-1792), was a native of Truro, and received his education at Cambridge. He practised at first as a physician, but afterwards took Orders, and became Chaplain to the Countess of Huntingdon. He was the author of a volume of hymns called *Carmina Christo or Hymns to the Saviour*, which was first published in 1792.

HEBER, Reginald (1783-1826), was born at Malpas in Cheshire, and educated at Brasenose College, Oxford. He had a distinguished University career, and his English Prize poem, *Palestine*, has a more than academic reputation. From 1807 to 1823 he was Rector of Hodnet, Shropshire, and in the latter year was appointed Bishop of Calcutta. He died suddenly at Trichinopoly, Southern India. He wrote a large number of excellent hymns.

HERBERT, George (1593-1632), the younger brother of Lord Herbert of Cherbury, was born at Montgomery. Having been educated at Westminster, he went to Cambridge and graduated at Trinity College. After some years spent in various employments at the University and the Court, he resolved to enter the Church. In 1630 he was presented to the living of Bemerton, near Salisbury, which he only lived to hold two years. His poems were not published until after his death. They are full of curious conceits, but also breathe a deep spirit of devotion. They soon acquired a great popularity, which they have always retained.

HERRICK, Robert (1519-1674), the descendant of an old Leicestershire family, was born in London. He was educated at St. John's College, Cambridge, took Orders, and became vicar of Dean Prior in Devonshire. He was ejected from his benefice during the Commonwealth, but regained it at the Restoration. He was the author of sacred as well as other poems, which were first printed in 1648.

HOLMES, Oliver Wendell, M.D., LL.D., son of the Rev. Abiel Holmes, D.D., of Cambridge, U.S.A., was born at Cambridge, August 9, 1809, and educated at Harvard, where he graduated in 1829. After practising for some time in Boston, he was elected in 1847 to the chair of Anatomy in Harvard. His writings in prose and verse are well known and widely circulated. They excel in humour and pathos. Although not strictly speaking a hymn-writer a few of his hymns are in extensive use.

HUGHES, Thomas, was born at Donnington Priory, near Newbury, Berks, 1823, and educated at Rugby, and at Oriel College, Oxford. He was called to the Bar, and in 1869 became a Queen's Counsel. From 1865 to 1868 he was M.P. for Lambeth, and from 1868–1874 for Frome. He has published several popular works, including *Tom Brown's School Days*, *Tom Brown at Oxford*, and others.

KEBLE, John (1792–1866), was born at Fairford in Gloucestershire. He was educated at Corpus Christi College, Oxford, and became a Fellow of Oriel College. In 1831 he succeeded Milman in the Professorship of Poetry, and in 1835 he was appointed to the living of Hursley, near Winchester. His principal work, *The Christian Year*, has enjoyed an extraordinary popularity, and has taken in this century the place which Watts and Wesley held in the last. He was one of the leaders of the so-called Tractarian movement.

KEN, Thomas (1637–1711), was born at Berkhampstead. He received his education at Winchester, and graduated at New College, Oxford, of which he became Fellow in 1657. His first living was at Brixton in the Isle of Wight, but soon afterwards he became Chaplain successively to the Princess of Orange at the Court of the Hague, and to Lord Dartmouth on his mission to Tangiers. In 1684 he was appointed by Charles II to the Bishopric of Bath and Wells, and in 1688 he was one of the seven bishops who were sent to the Tower. At the Revolution he refused to take the oath to William, and was in consequence deprived of his see. He took up his residence at Longleat, and there died in 1711. According to his own wish, he was buried at Frome 'just at sunrising.' He wrote much both in prose and verse. The familiar Morning and Evening Hymns form part of a Manual of Prayers for the use of the scholars of Winchester. The Evening Hymn is largely taken from some lines at the end of Sir T. Browne's *Religio Medici* (part ii. sect. 12).

LYTE, Henry Francis (1793–1847), was born at Ednam, near Kelso, and educated at Portora (the Royal School of Enniskillen), and at Trinity College, Dublin, where he graduated in 1814. At one time he had intended studying Medicine; but this he abandoned for Theology, and took Holy Orders in 1815. In 1823 he was made curate of Lower Brixham, Devon, where he remained twenty-four years. Failing health then compelled him to go abroad, but he died shortly after at Nice. His well known hymn, 'Abide with me,' was written two months only before his death.

MANT, Richard (1776–1848), was born at Southampton. He was educated at Winchester and Trinity College, Oxford, and in 1798 was elected a Fellow of Oriel. He became successively Bishop of Killaloe, Down and Connor, and Dromore. As a sacred poet, as well as a theological expositor, Bishop Mant gained great and deserved distinction.

MARCKANT, John, was incumbent of Clacton Magna in 1559, and of Stopland in 1563–8. He is known only as the author of one or two small pieces: a political poem on Lord Wentworth; a New Year's Gift entitled, *With speed return to God*, and *Verses to Divers Good Purposes*.

MARRIOTT, John (1780–1825), was born in

Leicestershire and educated at Christ Church, Oxford. His name appeared in the earliest Class List, which was issued at Oxford in 1802. For many years he held a living in Warwickshire, but afterwards removed to the neighbourhood of Exeter. The hymn by which he is chiefly remembered, 'Thou, whose Almighty word,' is the only one which he is known to have composed.

MERRICK, John (1720-1769), was born at Reading and educated at the Grammar School of the town. He was a Scholar of Trinity College, Oxford, and became Fellow of that society in 1714. He took Orders, but owing to ill health never held any preferment. His life was uneventful, and chiefly passed in study and literary labour. He was the author of numerous works, both in poetry and prose, including a Metrical Version of the Psalms which once had a considerable reputation.

MILMAN, Henry Hart (1791-1868), was born in London, and received his education at Eton and at Brasenose College, Oxford. In 1821 he was appointed to the Professorship of Poetry at Oxford, and in 1849 he became Dean of St. Paul's. He is remembered not only as an eminent historical writer, but also as a considerable poet.

MILTON, John (1608-1674), was born in Bread Street, Cheapside, and was educated at St. Paul's School and at Christ's College, Cambridge. From 1632-1638 he resided at his father's country-house at Horton in Buckinghamshire, and in the latter year he travelled in Italy. He returned to England on the approach of the Civil War, and took up his residence in London. In 1649 he was made Latin Secretary to the Council, and remained in that employment until the Restoration. In 1652 a failure of sight, which had long threatened him, developed into total blindness. His life was spared at the Restoration, and he devoted the remainder of his days 'in darkness and solitude' to the composition of his two great poems. He died in 1674, and was buried in St. Giles', Cripplegate. The 'Paraphrases on Psalms cxiv and cxxxvi' were written 'at fifteen years old,' although they were not published until 1645. The lines, 'Ring out, ye crystal spheres,' are stanzas xiii-xv of the 'Ode on the Nativity' (1629).

MONSELL, John Samuel Bewley (1811-1875), son of Thomas B. Monsell, Archdeacon of Londonderry, was born at St. Columb's, Londonderry, and educated at Trinity College, Dublin. He took Holy Orders in 1834, and became rector of St. Nicholas', Guildford. He died in consequence of a fall from the roof of his church, which was in the course of rebuilding. His prose works include *Our New Vicar*, 1867.

NEWMAN, John Henry, D.D. (1801-1890), was born in London and educated at Ealing and at Trinity College, Oxford, where he graduated in Honours in 1820 and became a Fellow of Oriel in 1822. He took Holy Orders in 1824 and was appointed to St. Mary's, Oxford, in 1828. His association with Keble, Pusey, and others in what is known as the 'Oxford Movement,' as well as in the periodical publication of *Tracts for the Times*, are matters of history. In 1845 he was received into the Church of Rome, and in 1879 was created a Cardinal. He died at the Edgbaston Oratory, Birmingham.

NEW VERSION, The, of the Psalms, was written by Nahum Tate and the Rev.

Nicholas Brady. It does not appear to be known what part they respectively took in the work. The first edition was published in 1696.

TATE, Nahum (1652-1715), was the son of an Irish clergyman, who suffered in the rebellion of 1641. After having been educated at Trinity College, Dublin, he went to London, where he made the acquaintance of Dryden. He was appointed poet-laureate in 1691, and was the author of some tragedies and miscellaneous poems. In addition to the metrical Psalms which he contributed to the New Version, he wrote some of the Hymns in the Appendix, including the well-known 'While shepherds watched their flocks by night.'

BRADY, Nicholas (1659-1726), was born at Bandon in Ireland. He was educated at Westminster School and at Christ Church, Oxford, and subsequently graduated at Trinity College, Dublin. During the war in Ireland he supported the cause of William, and, having done some service to the town of Bandon, was sent by the inhabitants to England with a petition requesting compensation for damages received during the campaign. He became popular in London by his preaching, and was presented to the Church of St. Catherine Cree, in the City. He afterwards held livings in the suburbs at Richmond and Clapham, and was also for a short time Vicar of Stratford-on-Avon.

OLD VERSION, The, of the Psalms, was the joint work of several authors. The first edition was undated, and dedicated to King Edward VI, and contains nineteen Psalms rendered into English verse by Thomas Sternhold. A second edition appeared in 1549, and a complete edition in 1562, together with the tunes. This is commonly known as *Day's Psalter*, from the name of the printer. The remaining Psalms were composed by John Hopkins, William Whittingham, John Pullain, E. G. (probably Edmund Grindal), D. (Richard) Cox, Thomas Becon, John Marckant, William Kethe and John Craig.

OLIVERS, Thomas 1725-1799, was born at Tregonan in Montgomeryshire. He was apprenticed to a shoemaker, but fell into disgrace and left his employment. While wandering about the country he happened to hear Whitefield preach at Bristol, and this circumstance led to an entire reformation of his life. He joined the Methodists, and, becoming acquainted with Wesley, was employed by him as an itinerant preacher. He died in London, and was interred in Wesley's grave. His celebrated hymn, 'The God of Abraham praise,' is said to have been suggested by a Hebrew melody, which he once heard in a London synagogue.

OSLER, Edward (1798-1863), was born at Falmouth, and was educated there for the medical profession, and then at Guy's Hospital, London. From 1819 to 1836 he was house-surgeon at Swansea Infirmary. He then removed to London and devoted himself to literary pursuits. In 1841 he became editor of the *Royal Cornwall Gazette*, and took up his residence at Truro, where he remained till his death. The hymn in this collection, 'O God, unseen yet ever near,' was one of a number he contributed to a religious periodical.

PIERPOINT, Folliot Sandford, was born at Bath, 1835, and educated at Queens' College, Cambridge, graduating in Classical

Honours in 1871. He has published several works, and has also contributed hymns to the *Churchman's Companion*, the most widely-known being, 'For the beauty of the earth.'

PROCTER, Adelaide Anne (1825-1864), daughter of Bryan Waller Procter (Barry Cornwall), was born in London. In 1851 she joined the Roman communion. Miss Procter displayed more than usual intellectual powers at an early age. In later years she was skilled in music and languages. Her principal work is *Legends and Lyrics*. She died in London.

'SCOTCH PARAPHRASES,' The, include a metrical version of the Psalms and some passages of Scripture rendered into verse. The Psalms were prepared by a committee of the General Assembly appointed in 1646, who used chiefly the poetical translation made by Francis Rouse, Provost of Eton. Rouse himself had drawn largely upon a previous version, which had been composed by Sir William Alexander at the request of James I. The Scripture Paraphrases were arranged in their present form by various committees of the Assembly between 1745 and 1781.

STANLEY, Arthur Penrhyn, D.D. (1815-1881), born at Alderley, Cheshire, was the son of Edward Stanley, Bishop of Norwich. He was educated at Rugby under Dr. Arnold. In 1834 he went up to Oxford, having won a Balliol scholarship, and commenced a career of unusual brilliancy at the University. In 1863 he was made Dean of Westminster, and married the same year Lady Augusta Bruce, a sister of Lord Elgin, and a personal friend and attendant of Queen Victoria. He died at the Deanery on July 18, 1881.

TOKE, Emma (1812-1878), daughter of John Leslie, D.D., Bishop of Kilmore, was born at Holywood, Belfast, and was married to the Rev. Nicholas Toke, Godington Park, Kent. Mrs. Toke's early hymns were written in 1851, 'at the request of a friend who was collecting for the Committee of the Society for the Promotion of Christian Knowledge.'

TOPLADY, Augustus Montague (1740-1778), was born at Farnham in Surrey. He was educated at Westminster School, and afterwards became a member of Trinity College, Dublin. Having taken Orders he was appointed vicar of Broad Hembury in Devon. In 1775 he resigned his living, and went to London, where he died three years later. He was a strong Calvinist, and a great opponent of Wesley. Besides some controversial and devotional works, he published, in 1776, *A Collection of Hymns for Public and Private Worship*.

TWELLS, Henry, was born in 1823, and educated at St. Peter's College, Cambridge. He took Holy Orders in 1849. In 1856 he became Head Master of Godolphin School, Hammersmith, and in 1873 Select Preacher at Cambridge. He was made an Honorary Canon of Peterborough in 1884. Canon Twells is best known by his beautiful evening hymn, 'At even, ere the sun was set.'

VAUGHAN, Henry (1621-1693), was born at Skethiog on Usk in Brecknockshire. He received his early education from a local clergyman, and afterwards became a member of Jesus College, Oxford. Subsequently he studied medicine and practised for a while as a physician at Brecon; but finally settled at his native place, where he spent the remainder of his life in seclusion. His poems, which were little known in his own day, and quite forgotten in the last century, have only received their due meed of appreciation in our own time.

WALLER, Edmund (1605-1687), was born at Coleshill in Hertfordshire, and was educated at Eton, and at King's College, Cambridge. He was a nephew of Hampden, and took the Parliamentary side at the beginning of the Civil War. In 1643 he joined in a Royalist plot, and was banished from the kingdom, but was allowed to return by Cromwell. He lived into the reign of James II, and died at Beaconsfield in his eighty-second year.

WATTS, Isaac (1674-1748), was the son of a schoolmaster at Southampton. He was educated there under a private tutor and at a Dissenting academy in London. He became minister to a London congregation, but his health, which had been injured by excessive study, soon gave way. In 1712 he retired to the residence of Sir Thomas Abney, at Newington, where he remained until his death. His works are very numerous, and include both educational and religious treatises. His hymns have probably been the most familiar and widely known of all English sacred poems.

WESLEY, Charles (1708-1788), was born at Epworth, educated at Westminster School, and at Christ Church, Oxford. He went with his brother John to Georgia, and returned to England in 1736. He afterwards aided his brother in the formation of the Methodist society, although in some particulars he differed from him. He wrote an immense number of hymns—more, perhaps, of great excellence than any other single writer. He was the father of Samuel Sebastian Wesley, the well-known organist and composer.

WESLEY, John (1703-1791), was born at his father's parsonage at Epworth, in Lincolnshire. He was educated at the Charterhouse, and at Christ Church, Oxford. In 1726 he was elected Fellow of Lincoln College, and for the next two years acted as curate to his father. He then returned to Oxford, and joined a small religious society, which had been formed by his brother Charles and a few friends, afterwards called by the derisive name of 'Methodists.' In 1735 he was sent out to the newly founded colony of Georgia, but fell into disputes with the colonists, and after an interval of two years came back to England. Later on he went to Germany in order to visit the Moravian settlements, having come under the influence of some Moravians while in Georgia. In 1738 he began to preach in London, and the remaining fifty-three years of his life were occupied chiefly in the organization of the Methodist Church. Besides his various works on religious and controversial subjects, filling thirty-two volumes, he wrote several excellent hymns, which were published with those of his brother.

WHITING, William (1825-1868), was born at Kensington, London. He was for many years Master of the Choir School at Winchester. His hymn, 'Eternal Father, strong to save,' was originally contributed to *Hymns Ancient and Modern*.

WILLIAMS, William (1717-1791), was born near Llandovery. He at first studied medicine, but gave up that pursuit in order to enter the Church. After he had taken Deacon's orders he joined the Calvinistic Methodist body, and spent the remainder of his life as an itinerant preacher. He wrote a great number of hymns both in Welsh and English.

WITHER, George (1588-1667), was born at Bentworth in Hampshire, and educated at Magdalen College, Oxford. He took an active part in the Civil War on the side of the Parliament, and after the Restoration was imprisoned for some years in the Tower. He died in London, and was buried in the Savoy. His works, which are very numerous, include two volumes of sacred verse, the *Hallelujah*, and the *Hymns and Songs of the Church*.

INDEX OF HYMNS SUITABLE FOR FESTIVALS AND SEASONS

MORNING.

HYMN
- 22. Awake, my soul, and with the sun.
- 58. Christ, Whose glory fills the skies.
- 60. Forth in Thy Name, O Lord, I go.
- 96. New every morning is the love.
- 153. Come, my soul, thou must be waking.
- 163. Jam lucis orto sidere.
- 164. Ales diei nuntius.

EVENING.

- 23. Glory to Thee, my God, this night.
- 97. Sun of my soul, Thou Saviour dear.
- 100. Abide with me.
- 122. At even, ere the sun was set.
- 135. The sun is sinking fast.

ADVENT.

- 52. Hark the glad sound!
- 64. Lo! He comes! with clouds descending.
- 86. The Lord will come! the earth shall quake!
- 136. That day of wrath, that dreadful day.
- 140. Great God, what do I see and hear!

HYMN
- 156. On Jordan's bank the Baptist's cry.
- 165. Nox et tenebrae et nubila.
- 169. Dies irae, dies illa.

CHRISTMAS.

- 24. While shepherds watched their flocks by night.
- 33. Christians, awake, salute the happy morn.
- 61. Hark! the herald angels sing.
- 146. All my heart this night rejoices.

EPIPHANY.

- 157. What star is this, with beams so bright.
- 168. Jesu dulcis memoria.

LENT.

- 6. O Lord, turn not Thy face from me.
- 38. When rising from the bed of death.
- 48. From lowest depths of woe.
- 75. O for a closer walk with God.
- 91. Just as I am, without one plea.
- 94. O Help us, Lord! each hour of need.
- 101. Far from my heavenly home.

HYMNS FOR FESTIVALS AND SEASONS.

PASSIONTIDE.

HYMN
29. When I survey the wondrous Cross.
131. O Sacred Head, surrounded.

EASTER.

130. Jesus Christ is risen to-day.
134. The strife is o'er, the battle done.
155. O risen Lord! O conqu'ring King!
160. Jesus lives! no longer now.

ASCENSION DAY.

19. The eternal gates lift up their heads.
116. Thou art gone up on high.
118. He is gone: beyond the skies.
129. The Lord ascendeth up on high.

WHITSUNDAY.

82. Our blest Redeemer, ere He breathed.
99. When God of old came down from heaven.
166. Veni, Creator Spiritus.
167. Veni, Sancte Spiritus.

TRINITY SUNDAY.

85. Holy, holy, holy, Lord God Almighty!

HOLY COMMUNION.

HYMN
53. My God, and is Thy Table spread.
103. O God, unseen yet ever near.
170. Lauda, Sion, Salvatorem.

MISSIONS.

44. To bless Thy chosen race.
84. Thou, Whose almighty word.

FOR THOSE AT SEA.

124. Eternal Father! strong to save.

HARVEST.

109. Lord of the Harvest, once again.

ALL SAINTS' DAY.

21. Jerusalem on high.
154. Who are these like stars appearing.

FESTIVAL OF MARTYRS.

87. The son of God goes forth to war.

END OF TERM.

47. Lord, dismiss us with Thy blessing.

ON page vi, in the list of acknowledgments, the name of J. R. Sterndale Bennett, Esq., should have been added after that of Otto Goldschmidt, Esq.

Hymns and Chorales.

PASSIONTIDE.

HYMN	
29.	When I survey the wondrous Cross.
131.	O Sacred Head, surrounded.

EASTER.

130.	Jesus Christ is risen to-day.
134.	The strife is o'er, the battle done.
155.	O risen Lord! O conqu'ring King!
160.	Jesus lives! no longer now.

HOLY COMMUNION.

HYMN	
53.	My God, and is Thy Table spread.
103.	O God, unseen yet ever near.
170.	Lauda, Sion, Salvatorem.

MISSIONS.

44.	To bless Thy chosen race.
84.	Thou, Whose almighty word.

FOR THOSE AT SEA

Hymns and Chorales

Hymn 1.

1.

YE that have spent the silent night
  In sleep and quiet rest,
And joy to see the cheerful light
  That riseth in the east;
Now lift your hearts, your voices raise,
  Your morning tribute bring,
And pay a grateful song of praise
  To Heaven's Almighty King.

And as this gloomy night did last
  But for a little space;
As heavenly day, now night is past,
  Doth show his pleasant face;
So let us hope, when faith and love
  Their work on earth have done,
God's blessed face to see above,
  Heaven's better, brighter Sun.

God grant us grace that height to gain,
  That glorious sight to see,
And send us, after worldly pain,
  A life from trouble free;
Where cheerful day shall ever shine,
  And sorrow never come;
Lord, be a place, a portion, mine,
  In that bright blissful home.

GEORGE GASCOIGNE, 1540-1577.

Hymn 2.

ST. CLEMENT DANES. DR. HOWARD, 1710-1782.

2.

PSALM XVIII.

O GOD, my strength and fortitude,
   Of force I must love Thee;
Thou art my castle and defence
   In my necessity:

My God, my rock in whom I trust,
   The worker of my wealth,
My refuge, buckler, and my shield,
   The horn of all my health.

I when beset with pain and grief
   Did pray to God for grace:
And He forthwith did hear my plaint
   Out of His holy place.

The Lord descended from above,
   And bowed the heavens on high:
And underneath His feet He cast
   The darkness of the sky;

On Cherubim and Seraphim
   Full royally He rode;
And on the wings of mighty winds
   Came flying all abroad.

Unspotted are the ways of God,
   His word is purely try'd;
He is a sure defence to such
   As in His faith abide.

For who is God, except the Lord?
   For other there is none:
Or who else is omnipotent,
   Saving our God alone?

The Old Version, 1562.

Hymn 3.

ST. STEPHEN. The Rev. W. Jones, 1726-1800.

3.

PSALM XXIII.

MY Shepherd is the living Lord,
    I therefore nothing need;
In pastures fair, near pleasant streams,
    He setteth me to feed.

He shall convert and glad my soul,
    And bring my mind in frame,
To walk in paths of righteousness,
    For His most holy Name.

Yea, though I walk the vale of death,
    Yet will I fear no ill;
Thy rod and staff they comfort me,
    And Thou art with me still.

Through all my life Thy favour is
    So frankly showed to me,
That in Thy house for evermore
    My dwelling-place shall be.

The Old Version, 1562.

Hymn 4.

NARENZA.
Ancient German Chorale, from Kölner Gesangbuch.

4.

PSALM XXV.

I LIFT my heart to Thee,
   My God and guide most just;
Now suffer me to take no shame,
   In Thee alone I trust.

Thy mercies manifold,
   Remember, Lord, I pray;
In pity Thou art plentiful,
   And so hast been alway.

Remember not the faults
   And frailty of my youth;
Call not to mind how ignorant
   I have been of Thy truth.

Nor after my deserts
   Let me Thy mercy find;
But of Thine own benignity,
   Lord, have me in Thy mind.

The Old Version, 1561.

Hymn 5.

THE OLD 100TH.   Day's Psalter, 1562.

5.

PSALM C.

ALL people that on earth do dwell,
 Sing to the Lord with cheerful voice;
Him serve with fear, His praise forth tell,
Come ye before Him and rejoice.

The Lord, ye know, is God indeed;
Without our aid He did us make:
We are His flock, He doth us feed,
And for His sheep He doth us take.

O enter then His gates with praise,
Approach with joy His courts unto;
Praise, laud, and bless His Name always,
For it is seemly so to do.

For why? the Lord our God is good,
His mercy is for ever sure;
His truth at all times firmly stood,
And shall from age to age endure.

The Old Version, 1562.

Hymn 6.

EATINGTON. DR. WILLIAM CROFT, 1677-1727.

6.

O LORD, turn not Thy face from me,
   Who lie in woful state,
Lamenting all my sinful life,
   Before Thy mercy-gate:

A gate which opens wide to those
   That do lament their sin;
Shut not that gate against me, Lord,
   But let me enter in.

And call me not to strict account
   How I have sojourned here:
For then my guilty conscience knows
   How vile I shall appear.

So come I to Thy mercy-gate,
   Where mercy doth abound,
Imploring pardon for my sin,
   To heal my deadly wound.

Mercy, good Lord, mercy I ask,
   This is the total sum;
For mercy, Lord, is all my suit,
   O let thy mercy come!

J. MARKANT, *circa* 1560.

Hymn 7.

OLD 137TH. Day's Psalter, 1563.

(14)

7.

BEHOLD the sun, that seem'd but now
    Enthronèd overhead,
Beginneth to decline below
    The globe whereon we tread;
And he, whom yet we look upon
    With comfort and delight,
Will quite depart from hence anon,
    And leave us to the night.

Thus time, unheeded, steals away
    The life which nature gave;
Thus are our bodies every day
    Declining to the grave:
Thus from us all our pleasures fly
    Whereon we set our heart;
And when the night of death draws nigh,
    Thus will they all depart.

Lord! though the sun forsake our sight,
    And mortal hopes are vain;
Let still Thine everlasting light
    Within our souls remain!
And in the nights of our distress
    Vouchsafe those rays divine,
Which from the Sun of Righteousness
    For ever brightly shine.

G. WITHER, 1588-1667

Hymn 8.

8.

COME, O come, in pious lays
    Sound we God Almighty's praise;
Hither bring, in one consent,
Heart, and voice, and instrument.
Let those things which do not live,
In still music praises give;
Nor a creature dumb be found
That hath either voice or sound.

Come, ye sons of human race,
In this chorus take your place:
And amid the mortal throng,
Be ye masters of the song.
Let, in praise of God, the sound
Run a never-ending round,
That our song of praise may be
Everlasting, as is He.

So this huge wide orb we see
Shall one choir, one temple be,
And our song shall over-climb
All the bounds of place and time,
And ascend from sphere to sphere
To the great Almighty's ear.
Then O come, in pious lays,
Sound we God Almighty's praise.

G. WITHER, 1588-1667.

Hymn 9.

CHORALE.
Freylinghausen's Gesangbuch, 1704.

9.

In the time of my distress
    When temptations me oppress,
And when I my sins confess,
    Sweet Spirit, comfort me.

When I lie within my bed,
Sick in heart, and sick in head,
And with doubts discomforted,
    Sweet Spirit, comfort me.

When the house doth sigh and weep,
And the world is drowned in sleep,
Yet mine eyes the watch do keep,
    Sweet Spirit, comfort me.

When the judgment is revealed,
And that opened which was sealed,
When to Thee I have appealed,
    Sweet Spirit, comfort me.

R. Herrick, 1591-1674

Hymn 10.

ABRIDGE.   Isaac Smith, *d.* 1800.

10.

PSALM XXIII.

THE God of Love my Shepherd is,
   And He That doth me feed:
While He is mine, and I am His,
   What can I want or need?

He leads me to the tender grass,
   Where I both feed and rest;
Then to the streams that gently pass:
   In both I have the best.

Or, if I stray, He doth convert
   And bring my mind in frame;
And all this not for my desert,
   But for His Holy Name.

Yea, in death's shady black abode
   Well may I walk, nor fear;
For Thou art with me, and Thy rod
   To guide, Thy staff to bear.

Surely Thy sweet and wondrous love
   Shall measure all my days;
And, as it never shall remove,
   So neither shall my praise!

G. HERBERT, 1593–1633.

Hymn 11.

MELCOMBE. SAMUEL WEBBE, sen., 1740-1817.

11.

COME, Holy Ghost, our souls inspire,
  And lighten with celestial fire:
Thou the anointing Spirit art,
Who dost Thy sevenfold gifts impart.

Thy blessed unction from above
Is comfort, life, and fire of love:
Enable with perpetual light
The dulness of our blinded sight.

Anoint and cheer our soiled face
With the abundance of Thy grace:
Keep far our foes; give peace at home:
Where Thou art guide no ill can come.

Teach us to know the Father, Son,
And Thee of Both, to be but One:
That, through the ages all along,
This may be our endless song.

Bishop Cosin, 1595–1671.

Hymn 12.

DOVER. ORLANDO GIBBONS, 1583-1625.

12.

THE seas are quiet when the winds give o'er,
    So calm are we when passions are no more:
For then we know how vain it was to boast
Of fleeting things, so certain to be lost:
Clouds of affection from our younger eyes
Conceal that emptiness which age descries.

The soul's dark cottage, battered and decayed,
Lets in new light through chinks that time has made:
Stronger by weakness, wiser men become,
As they draw near to their eternal home;
Leaving the old, both worlds at once they view,
That stand upon the threshold of the new.

E. WALLER, 1605–1687.

Hymn 13.

VIENNA. T. H. KNECHT, 1752-1817.

13.

PSALM CXXXVI.

LET us, with a gladsome mind,
   Praise the Lord, for He is kind:
  For His mercies aye endure,
  Ever faithful, ever sure.

Let us bless His name abroad,
For of gods He is the God:
  For His, &c.

Oh, let us His praises tell,
Who doth the wrathful tyrants quell:
  For His, &c.

Who with His miracles doth make
Amazèd heaven and earth to shake:
  For His, &c.

Who by His wisdom did create
The painted heavens so full of state:
  For His, &c.

Who did the solid earth ordain
To rise above the watery plain:
  For His, &c.

Who, by His all-commanding might,
Did fill the new-made world with light:
  For His, &c.

And caused the golden tressèd sun
All the day long his course to run:
  For His, &c.

The hornèd moon to shine by night,
Amongst her spangled sisters bright:
  For His, &c.

All living creatures He doth feed,
And with full hand supplies their need:
  For His, &c.

Let us therefore warble forth
His mighty majesty and worth:
  For His, &c.

That His mansion hath on high
Above the reach of mortal eye:
  For His mercies aye endure,
  Ever faithful, ever sure.

J. MILTON, 1608-1674

Hymn 14.

OSGARTHORPE. J. TUTIN.

Ring out, ye crys-tal spheres, Once bless our hu-man ears, If ye have power to touch our sen-ses so,) And let your sil-ver chime Move in me-lo-dious time; And let the base of heaven's deep or-gan blow;

For if such ho-ly song En-wrap our fan-cy long, Time will run back, and fetch the age of gold; And speck-led van-i-ty Will sick-en soon and die, And lep-rous sin will melt from earth-ly mould;

Yea, truth and jus-tice then Will down re-turn to men, Orbed in a rain-bow; and, like glo-ries wearing, Mer-cy will sit be-tween, Throned in ce-les-tial sheen, With ra-diant feet the tis-sued clouds down bearing;

blow: And with your nine-fold har-mo-ny Make up full con-sort to the an-gel-ic sym-pho-ny.
mould; And hell it-self will pass a-way, And leave her dolor-ous man-sions to the peer-ing day.
steering; And heaven, as at some fes-ti-val, Will o-pen wide the gates of her high pal-ace hall.

Whether we sleep or wake,
To Thee we both resign;
By night we see, as well as day,
If Thy light on us shine.

Whether we live or die,
Both we submit to Thee;
In death we live, as well as life,
If Thine in death we die.

J. AUSTIN, 1613-1669.

Hymn 15.

15.

BLEST be Thy love, dear Lord,
 That taught us this sweet way,
Only to love Thee for Thyself,
 And for that love obey.

O Thou, our souls' chief hope!
 We to Thy mercy fly:
Where'er we are, Thou canst protect,
 Whate'er we need, supply.

Whether we sleep or wake,
 To Thee we both resign;
By night we see, as well as day,
 If Thy light on us shine.

Whether we live or die,
 Both we submit to Thee;
In death we live, as well as life,
 If Thine in death we die.

J. AUSTIN, 1613-1669.

Hymn 16.

CULBACH. TÖPLER'S *Old Choral Melodies.*

16.

HARK, my soul, how everything
 Strives to serve our bounteous King:
Each a double tribute pays,
Sings its part, and then obeys.

Nature's chief and sweetest quire
Him with cheerful notes admire;
Chanting every day their lauds,
While the grove their song applauds.

Though their voices lower be,
Streams have, too, their melody;
Night and day they warbling run,
Never pause, but still sing on.

All the flowers that gild the spring
Hither their still music bring;
If Heaven bless them, thankful they
Smell more sweet, and look more gay.

Only we can scarce afford
This short office to our Lord;
We, on whom His beauty flows,
All things gives, and nothing owes.

Wake, for shame, my sluggish heart,
Wake, and gladly sing thy part;
Learn of birds, and springs, and flowers,
How to use thy nobler powers.

J Austin, 1613-1669.

Hymn 17.

ST. MARY or HACKNEY.　　　　　　　　　　Playford's Psalter, 1677.

NOW it belongs not to my care
   Whether I die or live;
To love and serve Thee is my share,
   And this Thy grace must give.

If death shall bruise this springing seed
   Before it come to fruit,
The will with Thee goes for the deed,
   Thy life was in the root.

Would I long bear my heavy load,
   And keep my sorrows long?
Would I long sin against my God,
   And His dear mercy wrong?

How much is sinful flesh my foe,
   That doth my soul pervert
To linger here in sin and woe,
   And steals from God my heart!

Christ leads me through no darker rooms
   Than He went through before;
He that unto God's Kingdom comes
   Must enter by this door.

Come, Lord, when grace hath made me meet
   Thy blessed face to see;
For if Thy work on earth be sweet,
   What will Thy glory be?

Then I shall end my sad complaints,
   And weary sinful days,
And join with the triumphant saints
   That sing Jehovah's praise.

My knowledge of that life is small;
   The eye of faith is dim;
But 'tis enough that Christ knows all,
   And I shall be with Him.

R. BAXTER, 1615-1691.

Hymn 18.

DARWELL'S 118TH.   THE REV. JOHN DARWELL, d. 1789.

18.

YE holy angels bright,
　　Who wait at God's right hand,
Or through the realms of light
　　Fly at your Lord's command,
　　　　Assist our song,
　　　　　　For else the theme
　　　　　　Too high doth seem
　　　　For mortal tongue.

Ye blessed souls at rest,
　　Who ran this earthly race,
And now, from sin released,
　　Behold the Saviour's face,
　　　　God's praises sound,
　　　　　　As, in his sight,
　　　　　　With sweet delight
　　　　Ye do abound.

Ye saints, who toil below,
　　Adore your heavenly King,
And, onward as ye go,
　　Some joyful anthems sing:
　　　　Take what He gives,
　　　　　　And praise Him still
　　　　　　Through good and ill,
　　　　Who ever lives.

My soul, bear thou thy part,
　　Triumph in God above;
And with a well-tuned heart
　　Sing thou the songs of love!
　　　　Let all thy days,
　　　　　　Till life shall end,
　　　　　　Whate'er He send,
　　　　Be filled with praise.

　　　　　　　　　　R. BAXTER, 1615-1691.

Hymn 19.

19.

THE eternal gates lift up their heads,
    The doors are open'd wide,
The King of Glory is gone up,
    Unto His Father's side.

Thou art gone in before us, Lord,
    Thou hast prepared a place,
That we may be where now Thou art,
    And look upon Thy face.

And ever on our earthly path
    A gleam of glory lies,
A light still breaks behind the cloud
    That veils Thee from our eyes.

Lift up our hearts, lift up our minds,
    And let Thy grace be given,
That while we linger yet below,
    Our treasure be in Heaven.

That, where Thou art at God's right hand,
    Our hope, our love may be;
Dwell in us now, that we may dwell
    For evermore in Thee.

Psalter, 1071.

Hymn 20.

GLOUCESTER. Ravenscroft's Psalter, 1621.

20.

PSALM CXXI.

UP to those bright and gladsome hills,
    Whence all my help is given,
I look and sigh for Him who fills,
    Unseen, both earth and heaven.

He is alone my help and hope,
    That I shall not be moved;
His watchful eye is ever ope,
    And guardeth His beloved.

The glorious God is my sole stay,
    He is my sun and shade:
The cold by night, the heat by day,
    Neither shall me invade.

He keeps me safe from every ill,
    Doth all my foes control:
He is a shield, and shelter still,
    Unto my very soul.

Whether abroad, amidst the crowd,
    Or else within my door,
He is my pillar and my cloud,
    Now and for evermore.

                          H. VAUGHAN, 1621-1695.

Hymn 21.

GOPSAL. G. F. HANDEL, 1684-1759.

21.

JERUSALEM on high
  My song and city is,
My home whene'er I die,
  The centre of my bliss:
    O happy place!
      When shall I be,
      My God, with Thee,
      To see Thy face?

Thy walls, sweet city, thine,
  With pearls are garnishèd;
Thy gates with praises shine,
  Thy streets with gold are spread:
    O happy, &c.

No sun by day shines there,
  No moon by silent night:
O no! these needless are:
  The Lamb's the city's Light:
    O happy, &c.

There dwells my Lord, my King,
  Judged here unfit to live;
There angels to Him sing,
  And lowly homage give:
    O happy, &c.

The Patriarchs of old
  There from their travels cease;
The Prophets there behold
  Their longed-for Prince of Peace:
    O happy, &c.

The Lamb's Apostles there
  I might with joy behold,
The Harpers I might hear
  Harping on harps of gold:
    O happy, &c.

No tears from any eyes
  Drop in that holy quire;
But Death itself there dies,
  And sighs themselves expire:
    O happy, &c.

There should temptation cease,
  My frailties there should end:
There should I rest in peace
  In the arms of my best friend:
    O happy place!
      When shall I be,
      My God, with Thee,
      To see Thy face?

S. CROSSMAN,

Hymn 22.

OLD TEN COMMANDMENTS TUNE. *Genevan Psalter*, 1561.

22.

Part I.

AWAKE, my soul, and with the sun
Thy daily stage of duty run;
Shake off dull sloth, and joyful rise
To pay thy morning sacrifice.

Thy precious time mis-spent redeem;
Each present day thy last esteem;
Improve thy talent with due care;
For the great day thyself prepare.

In conversation be sincere;
Keep conscience as the noontide clear;
Think how all-seeing God thy ways
And all thy secret thoughts surveys.

Wake and lift up thyself, my heart,
And with the angels bear thy part,
Who, all night long, unwearied sing
High praise to the Eternal King.

Part II.

All praise to Thee, who safe has kept,
And hast refresh'd me whilst I slept!
Grant, Lord, when I from death shall wake,
I may of endless light partake!

Lord, I my vows to Thee renew;
Disperse my sins as morning dew;
Guard my first springs of thought and will,
And with Thyself my spirit fill.

Direct, control, suggest, this day,
All I design, or do, or say;
That all my powers, with all their might,
In Thy sole glory may unite.

BISHOP KEN, 1637-1711.

Hymn 23.

TALLIS'S CANON. T. TALLIS, d. 1585.

23.

GLORY to Thee, my God, this night
For all the blessings of the light;
Keep me, O keep me, King of kings,
Beneath Thine own Almighty wings.

Forgive me, Lord, for Thy dear Son,
The ill that I this day have done,
That with the world, myself, and Thee,
I, ere I sleep, at peace may be.

Teach me to live that I may dread
The grave as little as my bed;
Teach me to die, that so I may
Rise glorious at the awful day.

O may my soul on Thee repose,
And may sweet sleep mine eyelids close,
Sleep that shall me more vigorous make
To serve my God when I awake.

When in the night I sleepless lie,
My soul with heavenly thoughts supply;
Let no ill dreams disturb my rest,
No powers of darkness me molest.

Praise God, from Whom all blessings flow,
Praise Him, all creatures here below,
Praise Him above, Angelic host,
Praise Father, Son, and Holy Ghost.

BISHOP KEN, 1637-1711.

Hymn 24.

WINCHESTER. *Alison's Psalter*, 1599.
Original Setting.

24.

WHILE shepherds watched their flocks by night,
    All seated on the ground,
The Angel of the Lord came down,
    And glory shone around.

'Fear not,' said he; for mighty dread
    Had seized their troubled mind;
'Glad tidings of great joy I bring
    To you and all mankind.

'To you in David's town this day
    Is born of David's line
A Saviour, Who is Christ the Lord:
    And this shall be the sign:

'The heavenly Babe you there shall find
    To human view displayed,
All meanly wrapped in swathing bands,
    And in a manger laid.'

Thus spake the seraph; and forthwith
    Appeared a shining throng
Of Angels praising God, who thus
    Addressed their joyful song:

'All glory be to God on high,
    And on the earth be peace;
Good will henceforth from heaven to men
    Begin and never cease.'

NAHUM TATE 1652-1715.

Hymn 25.

118TH PSALM. DR. CROFT, 1677-1727.

25.

PSALM LXXXIV.

LORD of the worlds above,
   How pleasant and how fair
The dwellings of Thy love,
   Thine earthly temples are!
     To Thine abode
    My heart aspires,
    With warm desires
     To see my God.

O happy souls that pray
   Where God appoints to hear!
O blessed those that pay
   Their constant service there!
     They praise Thee still;
    And happy they
    That love the way
     To Sion's hill.

They go from strength to strength
   Through this dark vale of tears,
Till each arrives at length,
   Till each in heaven appears:
     O glorious seat!
    When God our King
    Shall thither bring
     Our willing feet.

The Lord His people loves,
   His hand no good withholds
From those His heart approves,
   From pure and faithful souls:
     Thrice happy he,
    O God of Hosts,
    Whose spirit trusts
     Alone in Thee.

I. WATTS, 1674-1743.

Hymn 26.

26.

PSALM XC.

O GOD, our help in ages past,
   Our hope for years to come,
Our shelter from the stormy blast,
   And our eternal home:

Under the shadow of Thy throne
   Thy saints have dwelt secure,
Sufficient is Thine arm alone,
   And our defence is sure.

Before the hills in order stood,
   Or earth received her frame,
From everlasting Thou art God,
   To endless years the same.

A thousand ages in Thy sight
   Are like an evening gone;
Short as the watch that ends the night
   Before the rising sun.

Time, like an ever rolling stream,
   Bears all its sons away;
They fly forgotten, as a dream
   Dies at the opening day.

O God, our help in ages past,
   Our hope for years to come;
Be Thou our Guard while life shall last,
   And our eternal home!

I. Watts, 1674-1748.

Hymn 27.

THE OLD 100TH. *Day's Psalter, 1562.*

27.

PSALM C.

BEFORE Jehovah's awful throne,
  Ye nations, bow with sacred joy;
Know that the Lord is God alone,
He can create, and He destroy.

His sovereign power, without our aid,
Made us of clay, and formed us men;
And when, like wandering sheep, we strayed,
He brought us to His fold again.

We'll crowd Thy gates with thankful songs,
High as the heavens our voices raise:
And earth, with her ten thousand tongues,
Shall fill Thy courts with sounding praise.

Wide as the world is Thy command;
Vast as eternity Thy love;
Firm as a rock Thy truth shall stand
When rolling years have ceased to move.

I. WATTS, 1674-1748, *varied by* C. WESLEY.

Hymn 28.

LONDON NEW. Scotch Psalter, 1635.

28.

There is a land of pure delight,
  Where saints immortal reign,
Infinite day excludes the night,
  And pleasures banish pain.

There everlasting spring abides,
  And never-withering flowers:
Death, like a narrow sea, divides
  This heavenly land from ours.

O could we make our doubts remove,
  These gloomy doubts that rise,
And see the Canaan that we love
  With unbeclouded eyes!

Could we but climb where Moses stood,
  And view the landscape o'er,
Not Jordan's stream nor death's cold flood,
  Should fright us from the shore.

I. Watts, 1674–1748.

Hymn 29.

ROCKINGHAM. *Adapted by* E. MILLER, 1731-1807.

29.

WHEN I survey the wondrous Cross,
On which the Prince of Glory died,
My richest gain I count but loss,
And pour contempt on all my pride.

Forbid it, Lord, that I should boast
Save in the Cross of Christ my God:
All the vain things that charm me most
I sacrifice them to His blood.

See from His head, His hands, His feet,
Sorrow and love flow mingled down!
Did e'er such love and sorrow meet,
Or thorns compose so rich a crown?

Were the whole realm of nature mine,
That were a present far too small;
Love so amazing, so divine,
Demands my soul, my life, my all.

1. Watts, 1674–1748.

Hymn 30.

ST. MICHAEL. *Day's Psalter,* 1565.

30.

My soul, repeat His praise
  Whose mercies are so great,
Whose anger is so slow to rise,
  So ready to abate.

High as the heavens are raised
  Above the ground we tread,
So far the riches of His grace
  Our highest thoughts exceed.

His power subdues our sins;
  And his forgiving love,
Far as the east is from the west,
  Doth all our guilt remove.

The pity of the Lord
  To those that fear His Name,
Is such as tender parents feel;
  He knows our feeble frame.

Our days are as the grass,
  Or like the morning flower;
If one sharp blast sweep o'er the field,
  It withers in an hour.

But Thy compassions, Lord,
  To endless years endure;
And children's children ever find
  Thy words of promise sure.

I. Watts, 1674-1748.

Hymn 31.

ST. PANCRAS. T. BATTISHILL, 1738-1801.
(Original Setting.)

31.

COME, gracious Spirit, heavenly Dove,
  With light and comfort from above;
Be thou our Guardian, Thou our Guide;
O'er every thought and step preside.

The light of truth to us display,
And make us know and choose Thy way;
Plant holy fear in every heart,
That we from God may ne'er depart.

Lead us to holiness—the road
That we must take to dwell with God;
Lead us to Christ, the living Way,
Nor let us from His precepts stray.

Lead us to God, our final Rest,
To be with Him for ever blest;
Lead us to Heaven, its bliss to share,
Fulness of joy for ever there.

Adapted from SIMON BROWNE, 1720.

Hymn 32.

OLD 112TH.
MARTIN LUTHER, 1483-1546.

32.

ETERNAL God, of beings First,
   Of all created good the Spring,
For Thee I long, for Thee I thirst,
   My love, my Saviour, and my King!
Thine is a never-failing store;
If God be mine, I ask no more.

The fairest world of light on high
   Reflection makes but faint of Thine:
The glorious tenants of the sky
   In God's own beams transported shine:
But, should'st Thou wrap Thy face in shade,
Soon all their life and lustre fade.

Thy presence makes celestial day,
   And fills each raptured soul with bliss;
Night would prevail, were God away,
   And spirits pine in Paradise!
In vain would all the angels try
To fill Thy room, Thy lack supply.

And sure, from Heaven we turn our eyes
   In vain to seek for bliss below;
The tree of Life can't root nor rise,
   Nor in this blasted region grow:
The wealth of this poor barren clod
Can ne'er make up the want of God.

But, Lord, in Thee the thirsty soul
   Will meet with full, with rich supplies:
Thy smiles will all her fears control,
   Thy beauties feast her ravished eyes:
To failing flesh and fainting hearts
Thy favour life and strength imparts!

SIMON BROWNE, 1680-1732.

Hymn 33.

YORKSHIRE.   John Wainwright, d. 1768.

33.

CHRISTIANS, awake, salute the happy morn
Whereon the Saviour of the world was born;
Rise to adore the mystery of love,
Which hosts of angels chanted from above;
With them the joyful tidings first begun
Of God Incarnate, and the Virgin's Son.

Then to the watchful shepherds it was told,
Who heard the angelic herald's voice,
'Behold,
I bring glad tidings of a Saviour's birth
To you and all the nations upon earth;
This day hath God fulfilled His promised word,
This day is born a Saviour, Christ the Lord.'

He spake: and straightway the celestial choir
In hymns of joy, unknown before, conspire;
The praises of redeeming love they sang,
And heaven's whole orb with Hallelujahs rang:
God's highest glory was their anthem still,
Peace upon earth, and unto men goodwill.

O may we keep and ponder in our mind
God's wondrous love in saving lost mankind:
Trace we the Babe, who hath retrieved our loss,
From the poor manger to the bitter Cross.
Tread in His steps, assisted by His grace,
Till man's first heavenly state again takes place.

Then may we hope, the angelic hosts among,
To join, redeemed, a glad triumphant throng;
He that was born upon this joyful day
Around us all His glory shall display;
Saved by His love, unceasing we shall sing
Eternal praise to Heaven's Almighty King.

Hymn 34.

34.

How are Thy servants blest, O Lord,
    How sure is their defence!
Eternal Wisdom is their guide,
    Their help, Omnipotence.

From all my griefs and fears, O Lord,
    Thy mercy sets me free;
While in the confidence of prayer
    My heart takes hold of Thee.

In midst of dangers, fears, and death,
    Thy goodness I'll adore;
Still praise Thee for Thy mercies past,
    And humbly hope for more.

My life, while Thou preserv'st that life,
    Thy sacrifice shall be;
And O may death, when death shall come,
    Unite my soul to Thee!

J. Addison, 1672–1719.

Hymn 35.

WOBURN.

HENRY CAREY, d. 1743. Original harmonies composed for Addison's Paraphrase of Psalm xxiii.

35.

PSALM XXIII.

THE Lord my pasture shall prepare,
And feed me with a shepherd's care;
His presence shall my wants supply,
And guard me with a watchful eye;
My noonday walks He shall attend,
And all my midnight hours defend.

When in the sultry glebe I faint,
Or on the thirsty mountain pant,
To fertile vales and dewy meads
My weary, wandering steps He leads,
Where peaceful rivers, soft and slow,
Amid the verdant landscape flow.

Though in the paths of death I tread,
With gloomy horrors overspread,
My steadfast heart shall fear no ill,
For Thou, O Lord, art with me still:
Thy friendly crook shall give me aid,
And guide me through the dreadful shade.

J. Addison, 1672-1719.

Hymn 36.

CHORALE. *Freylinghausen's Gesangbuch*, 1704.

(72)

36.

PSALM XIX.

THE spacious firmament on high,
  With all the blue ethereal sky,
And spangled heavens, a shining frame,
Their great Original proclaim ;
The unwearied sun from day to day
Does his Creator's power display,
And publishes to every land
The work of an Almighty hand.

Soon as the evening shades prevail,
The moon takes up the wondrous tale,
And nightly to the listening earth
Repeats the story of her birth ;
Whilst all the stars that round her burn,
And all the planets in their turn,
Confirm the tidings as they roll,
And spread the truth from pole to pole.

What, though in solemn silence all
Move round the dark terrestrial ball ;
What, though no real voice nor sound
Amidst their radiant orbs be found ;
In reason's ear they all rejoice,
And utter forth a glorious voice,
For ever singing, as they shine,
'The hand that made us is Divine.'

J. Addison, 1672-1719.

Hymn 37.

FERRY. J. GREEN's Collection, 1724.

37.

WHEN all Thy mercies, O my God,
  My rising soul surveys,
Transported with the view, I'm lost
  In wonder, love, and praise.

Thy providence my life sustained
  And all my wants redrest,
When in the silent womb I lay,
  And hung upon the breast.

To all my weak complaints and cries
  Thy mercy lent an ear,
E'er yet my feeble thoughts had learnt
  To form themselves in prayer.

When in the slippery paths of youth
  With heedless steps I ran,
Thine arm unseen conveyed me safe
  And led me up to man.

Ten thousand thousand precious gifts
  My daily thanks employ;
Nor is the least a cheerful heart,
  That tastes those gifts with joy.

Through every period of my life
  Thy goodness I'll pursue;
And after death, in distant worlds
  The glorious theme renew.

J. Addison, 1672-1719.

Hymn 38.

WALSALL. Attributed to H. PURCELL, 1658–1695.

38.

WHEN rising from the bed of death,
    O'erwhelm'd with guilt and fear,
I see my Maker face to face,
    O how shall I appear?

If yet, while pardon may be found,
    And mercy may be sought,
My heart with inward horror shrinks,
    And trembles at the thought,

When Thou, O Lord, shalt stand disclos'd
    In majesty severe,
And sit in judgment on my soul,
    O how shall I appear?

But Thou hast told the troubled soul,
    Who does her sins lament,
The timely tribute of her tears
    Shall endless woe prevent.

Then see the sorrows of my heart,
    Ere yet it be too late,
And add my Saviour's dying groans
    To give those sorrows weight.

For never shall my soul despair
    Her pardon to procure,
Who knows Thy only Son has died
    To make that pardon sure.

J. ADDISON, 1672-1719.

Hymn 39.

BURFORD.　　　　　　　　　　Attributed to H. PURCELL, 1658-1695.

39.

PSALM VIII.

O THOU, to Whom all creatures bow
    Within this earthly frame,
Through all the world how great art Thou!
    How glorious is Thy name!

In heaven Thy wondrous acts are sung,
    Nor fully reckoned there;
And yet Thou mak'st the infant tongue
    Thy boundless praise declare.

Through Thee the weak confound the strong,
    And crush their haughty foes;
And so Thou quell'st the wicked throng,
    That Thee and Thine oppose.

What's man, (say I,) that, Lord, Thou lov'st
    To keep him in Thy mind?
Or what his offspring, that Thou prov'st
    To them so wondrous kind?

They jointly own his powerful sway;
    The beasts that prey or graze;
The bird that wings its airy way;
    And fish that cuts the seas.

O Thou to whom all creatures bow
    Within this earthly frame,
Through all the world how great art Thou!
    How glorious is Thy name!

The New Version, 1698.
(TATE, 1652-1715. BRADY, 1644-1726.)

Hymn 40.

CHICHESTER. Ravenscroft's Psalter, 1621.

40.

PSALM XXXIII.

LET all the just to God with joy
    Their cheerful voices raise,
For well the righteous it becomes
    To sing glad songs of praise.

By His Almighty word at first
    The heavenly arch was reared,
And all the beauteous hosts of light
    At His command appeared.

The swelling floods, together rolled,
    He makes in heaps to lie;
And lays, as in a storehouse, safe,
    The wat'ry treasures by.

Let earth and all that dwell therein
    Before Him trembling stand;
For when He spake the word 'twas made,
    'Twas fixed at His command.

Our soul on God with patience waits,
    Our help and shield is He;
Then, Lord, let still our hearts rejoice,
    Because we trust in Thee.

The riches of Thy mercy, Lord,
    Do Thou to us extend;
Since we for all we want or wish
    On Thee alone depend.

The New Version, 1698.

Hymn 41.

NOTTINGHAM or ST. MAGNUS.   JEREMIAH CLARK, 1670-1707.

41.

PSALM XXXIV.

THROUGH all the changing scenes of life,
  In trouble and in joy,
The praises of my God shall still
  My heart and tongue employ.

Of His deliverance I will boast,
  Till all that are distrest,
From my example comfort take,
  And charm their griefs to rest.

O magnify the Lord with me,
  With me exalt His Name;
When in distress to Him I called,
  He to my rescue came.

The hosts of God encamp around
  The dwellings of the just;
Deliverance He affords to all
  Who on His succour trust.

O make but trial of His love,
  Experience will decide
How blest are they, and only they,
  Who in His truth confide.

Fear Him, ye saints, and you will then
  Have nothing else to fear;
Make you His service your delight,
  Your wants shall be His care.

The New Version, 1693.

Hymn 42.

MARTYRDOM.   HUGH WILSON, 1764-1824.
(Original Setting.)

42.

PSALM XLII.

AS pants the hart for cooling streams
    When heated in the chase;
So longs my soul, O God, for Thee,
    And Thy refreshing grace.

For Thee, my God, the Living God,
    My thirsty soul doth pine:
O when shall I behold Thy face,
    Thou Majesty divine?

God of my strength, how long shall I,
    Like one forgotten, mourn?
Forlorn, forsaken, and exposed
    To my oppressor's scorn?

Why restless, why cast down, my soul?
    Hope still, and thou shalt sing
The praise of Him, who is Thy God,
    Thy health's eternal spring.

The New Version, 1696.

Hymn 43.

WALDECK. German Chorale. From *Old Church Psalmody*.

43.

PSALM LVII.

O GOD, my heart is fix'd, 'tis bent,
 Its thankful tribute to present;
And with my heart my voice I'll raise
To Thee, my God, in songs of praise.

Awake, my glory; harp and lute,
No longer let your strings be mute:
And I, my tuneful part to take,
Will with the early dawn awake.

Thy praises, Lord, I will resound
To all the list'ning nations round:
Thy mercy highest heav'n transcends,
Thy truth beyond the clouds extends.

Be Thou, O God, exalted high;
And, as Thy glory fills the sky,
So let it be on earth display'd,
Till Thou art here, as there, obey'd.

The New Version, 1698.

Hymn 44.

DONCASTER. S. WESLEY, 1766–1837.

44.

PSALM LXVII.

TO bless Thy chosen race,
    In mercy, Lord, incline;
And cause the brightness of Thy face
    On all Thy saints to shine.

That so Thy wondrous way
    May through the world be known;
Whilst distant lands their tribute pay,
    And Thy salvation own.

Let differing nations join
    To celebrate Thy fame;
Let all the world, O Lord, combine
    To praise Thy glorious Name.

O let them shout and sing,
    With joy and pious mirth,
For Thou, the righteous Judge and King,
    Shalt govern all the earth.

The New Version, 1696.

Hymn 45.

BEDFORD. W. WHEALL, d. 1745.

45.

PSALM LXXXIV.

O GOD of Hosts, the mighty Lord,
   How lovely is the place
Where Thou, enthroned in glory, show'st
   The brightness of Thy face!

My longing soul faints with desire
   To view Thy blest abode:
My panting heart and flesh cry out
   For Thee the living God.

Thrice happy they whose choice has Thee
   Their sure protection made;
Who long to tread the sacred ways
   That to Thy dwelling lead!

Thus they proceed from strength to strength,
   And still approach more near;
Till all on Sion's holy mount
   Before their God appear.

Thou God, Whom heavenly hosts obey,
   How highly blest is he
Whose hope and trust, securely placed,
   Is still reposed on Thee!

The New Version, 1696.

Hymn 46.

CHORALE. Swiss.

46.

PSALM XCI.

HE that has God his Guardian made,
   Shall under the Almighty's shade
Secure and undisturb'd abide.
Thus to my soul of Him I'll say,
He is my fortress and my stay,
   My God, in Whom I will confide.

His tender love and watchful care
Shall free thee from the fowler's snare,
   And from the noisome pestilence:
He over thee His wings shall spread,
And cover thy unguarded head;
   His truth shall be thy strong defence.

The New Version, 16.

Hymn 47.

ERFURT. KLUG's *Geistliche Lieder*, 1543.

47.

PSALM XCIII.

WITH glory clad, with strength arrayed,
    The Lord, that o'er all nature reigns,
The world's foundations strongly laid,
    And the vast fabric still sustains.

How surely stablished is Thy throne,
    Which shall no change or period see :
For Thou, O Lord, and Thou alone,
    Art God from all eternity.

The floods, O Lord, lift up their voice,
    And toss the troubled waves on high ;
But God above can still their noise,
    And make the angry sea comply.

Thy promise, Lord, is ever sure ;
    And they that in Thy house would dwell,
That happy station to secure
    Must still in holiness excel.

The New Version, 1696.

Hymn 48.

ST. BRIDE.
DR. S. HOWARD, 1710-1782.
(Original Setting.)

48.

PSALM CXXX.

FROM lowest depths of woe
    To God I sent my cry;
Lord, hear my supplicating voice,
    And graciously reply.

My soul with patience waits
    For Thee the living Lord;
My hopes are on Thy promise built,
    Thy never-failing word.

My longing eyes look out
    For Thy enlivening ray,
More duly than the morning watch
    To spy the dawning day.

Let Israel trust in God;
    No bounds His mercy knows,
The plenteous source and spring from whence
    Eternal succour flows:

Whose friendly streams to us
    Supplies in want convey;
A healing spring, a spring to cleanse,
    And wash our guilt away.

The New Version, 1698.

Hymn 49.

LONDON NEW. Scotch Psalter, 1635.

49.

PSALM CXIX.

FOR ever, and for ever, Lord,
    Unchang'd Thou dost remain:
Thy word establish'd in the heav'ns
    Does all their orbs sustain.

Thro' circling ages, Lord, Thy truth
    Immovable shall stand,
As does the earth, which Thou uphold'st
    By Thy Almighty hand.

All things the course by Thee ordain'd
    E'en to this day fulfil;
They are the faithful subjects all
    And servants of Thy will.

Unless Thy sacred law had been
    My comfort and delight,
I must have fainted, and expir'd
    In dark affliction's night.

Thy precepts therefore from my thoughts
    Shall never, Lord, depart;
For Thou by them hast to new life
    Restor'd my dying heart.

As I am Thine, entirely Thine,
    Protect me, Lord, from harm;
Who have Thy precepts sought to know
    And carefully perform.

I've seen an end of what we call
    . Perfection here below:
But Thy commandments, like Thyself,
    No change or period know.

The New Version, 1698.

Hymn 50.

CHORALE. JOHANN HERMANN SCHEIN, 1586-1630.

50.

PSALM CXXXIX.

THOU, Lord, by strictest search hast known
My rising up and lying down ;
My secret thoughts are known to Thee,
Known long before conceiv'd by me.

Thine eye my bed and path surveys,
My publick haunts and private ways ;
Thou know'st what 'tis my lips would vent,
My yet unutter'd words' intent.

Surrounded by Thy pow'r I stand,
On ev'ry side I find Thy hand :
O skill, for human reach too high !
Too dazzling bright for mortal eye !

O could I so perfidious be,
To think of once deserting Thee,
Where, Lord, could I Thy influence shun ?
Or whither from Thy presence run ?

If I the morning's wings could gain,
And fly beyond the western main,
Thy swifter hand would first arrive,
And there arrest Thy fugitive.

Or, should I try to shun Thy sight
Beneath the sable wings of night ;
One glance from Thee, one piercing ray,
Would kindle darkness into day.

The veil of night is no disguise,
No screen from Thy all-searching eyes ;
Through midnight shades Thou find'st Thy way,
As in the blazing noon of day.

Thou know'st the texture of my heart,
My reins, and ev'ry vital part ;
Each single thread in nature's loom
By Thee was cover'd in the womb.

I'll praise Thee, from whose hands I came,
A work of such a curious frame ;
The wonders Thou in me hast shown,
My soul with grateful joy must own.

Thine eyes my substance did survey,
While yet a lifeless mass it lay ;
In secret how exactly wrought,
Ere from its dark inclosure brought.

Let me acknowledge too, O God,
That, since this maze of life I trod,
Thy thoughts of love to me surmount
The pow'r of numbers to recount.

Far sooner could I reckon o'er
The sands upon the ocean's shore ;
Each morn, revising what I've done,
I find th' account but new begun.

Search, try, O God, my thoughts and heart,
If mischief lurks in any part ;
Correct me where I go astray,
And guide me in Thy perfect way.

The New Version, 1698.

Hymn 51.

118TH PSALM. DR. CROFT, 1677-1727.

PSALM CXLVIII.

YE boundless realms of joy,
   Exalt your Maker's fame,
His praise your song employ
  Above the starry frame;
    Your voices raise,
      Ye cherubim
      And seraphim,
    To sing His praise.

Thou moon, that rul'st the night,
  And sun, that guid'st the day:
Ye glittering stars of light,
  To Him your homage pay;
    His praise declare,
      Ye heavens above,
      And clouds that move
    In liquid air.

Let them adore the Lord,
  And praise His holy Name,
By Whose Almighty word
  They all from nothing came;
    And all shall last
      From changes free;
      His firm decree
    Stands ever fast.

To God the Father, Son,
  And Spirit, ever blest,
Eternal Three in One,
  All worship be addrest;
    As heretofore
      It was, is now,
      And shall be so
    For evermore.

The New Version, 1698.

Hymn 52.

BRISTOL.   Ravenscroft's Psalter, 1621.

52.

HARK, the glad sound! the Saviour comes,
 The Saviour promised long;
Let every heart prepare a throne,
 And every voice a song!

He comes, the prisoners to release,
 In Satan's bondage held;
The gates of brass before Him burst,
 The iron fetters yield.

He comes, from thickest films of vice
 To clear the mental ray,
And on the eye-balls of the blind
 To pour celestial day.

He comes, the broken heart to bind,
 The bleeding soul to cure,
And with the treasures of His grace
 To enrich the humble poor.

Our glad Hosannas, Prince of Peace,
 Thy welcome shall proclaim,
And heaven's eternal arches ring
 With Thy beloved Name.

P. Doddridge, 1702-1751.

Hymn 53.

ROCKINGHAM. *Adapted by* E. MILLER, 1731–1807.

53.

MY God, and is Thy Table spread,
And doth Thy Cup with love o'erflow?
Thither be all Thy children led,
And let them all Thy sweetness know.

Hail, sacred Feast, which Jesus makes,
Rich banquet of His Flesh and Blood !
Thrice happy he who here partakes
That sacred Stream, that heavenly Food.

Why are its dainties all in vain
Before unwilling hearts displayed?
Was not for them the Victim slain?
Are they forbid the children's Bread?

O let Thy Table honoured be,
And furnished well with joyful guests;
And may each soul salvation see,
That here its sacred pledges tastes.

To Father, Son, and Holy Ghost,
The God Whom heaven and earth adore,
From men and from the Angel-host
Be praise and glory evermore.

P. DODDRIDGE, 1702–1751.

Hymn 54.

54.

JESUS! Thy boundless love to me
   No thought can reach, no tongue declare;
O knit my thankful heart to Thee,
   And reign without a rival there:
Thine only, Thine alone, I am;
Lord, with Thy love my heart inflame!

O grant that nothing in my soul
   May dwell, but Thy pure love alone:
O may Thy love possess me whole,
   My joy, my treasure, and my crown:
All coldness from my heart remove,
May every act, word, thought, be love.

O Love! how cheering is thy ray!
   All pain before thy presence flies;
Care, anguish, sorrow, melt away,
   Where'er thy healing beams arise;
O Jesus, nothing may I see,
Nothing desire, or seek, but Thee.

In suffering, be Thy Love my peace;
   In weakness, be Thy Love my power:
And when the storms of life shall cease,
   Jesus, in that tremendous hour,
In death, as life, be Thou my Guide,
And save me, Who for me hast died.

J. WESLEY, 1703-1791.

Hymn 55.

STETERBURG. NICOLAUS DECIUS, d. 1541.

55.

LO! God is here! let us adore
   And own how dreadful is this place;
Let all within us feel His power,
   And silent bow before His face!
Who know His power, His grace who prove,
Serve Him with awe, with reverence love.

Lo! God is here! Him day and night
   The united quires of angels sing:
To Him enthroned above all height,
   Heaven's hosts their noblest praises bring;
Disdain not, Lord, our meaner song,
Who praise Thee with a stammering tongue.

Gladly the joys of earth we leave,
   Wealth, pleasure, fame, for Thee alone:
To Thee our will, soul, flesh, we give;
   O take, O seal them for Thine own!
Thou art the God! Thou art the Lord!
Be Thou by all Thy works adored!

Being of beings, may our praise
   Thy courts with grateful fragrance fill,
Still may we stand before Thy face,
   Still hear and do Thy sovereign will:
To Thee may all our thoughts arise,
Ceaseless, accepted sacrifice!

                    J. WESLEY, 1703-1791.

Hymn 56.

IRISH. Dublin Hymn Book, 1749.

56.

ALL praise to Him who dwells in bliss,
   Who made both day and night;
Whose throne is darkness, in th' abyss
   Of uncreated light!

Each thought and deed His piercing eyes
   With strictest search survey;
The deepest shades no more disguise
   Than the full blaze of day.

Whom Thou dost guard, O King of kings,
   No evil shall molest:
Under the shadow of Thy wings
   Shall they securely rest.

Thy angels shall around their beds
   Their constant stations keep;
Thy faith and truth shall shield their heads,
   For Thou dost never sleep.

May we, with calm and sweet repose,
   And heavenly thoughts refresh'd,
Our eyelids with the morn unclose,
   And bless the Ever-bless'd!

C. WESLEY, 1708-1788.

Hymn 57.

57.

COME, O Thou Traveller unknown,
　　Whom still I hold, but cannot see,
My company before is gone,
　　And I am left alone with Thee;
With Thee all night I mean to stay,
And wrestle till the break of day.

In vain Thou strugglest to get free,
　　I never will unloose my hold;
Art Thou the Man that died for me?
　　The secret of Thy love unfold.
Wrestling, I will not let Thee go,
Till I Thy Name, Thy Nature know.

Wilt Thou not yet to me reveal
　　Thy new, unutterable Name?
Tell me, I still beseech Thee, tell:
　　To know it now resolved I am:
Wrestling, I will not let Thee go,
Till I Thy Name, Thy Nature know.

My strength is gone; my nature dies;
　　I sink beneath Thy weighty hand,
Faint to revive, and fall to rise;
　　I fall, and yet by faith I stand:
I stand, and will not let Thee go,
Till I Thy Name, Thy Nature know.

Yield to me now, for I am weak,
　　But confident in self-despair;
Speak to my heart, in blessings speak,
　　Be conquer'd by my instant prayer!
Speak, or Thou never hence shall move,
And tell me, if Thy Name is Love?

'Tis Love! 'tis Love! Thou diedst for me!
　　I hear Thy whisper in my heart!
The morning breaks, the shadows flee;
　　Pure universal Love Thou art!
In vain I have not wept or strove;
Thy Nature, and Thy Name, is Love.

C. WESLEY, 1708-1788.

Hymn 58.

Choral. J. H. Chr. Bach. 1643-1703.

58.

CHRIST, Whose glory fills the skies,
    Christ, the true, the only Light,
Sun of Righteousness, arise,
    Triumph o'er the shades of night :
Day-spring from on high, be near :
Day-star, in my heart appear !

Dark and cheerless is the morn
    Unaccompanied by Thee ;
Joyless is the day's return,
    Till Thy mercy's beams I see ;
Till they inward light impart,
Glad my eyes, and warm my heart.

Visit then this soul of mine,
    Pierce the gloom of sin and grief,
Fill me, Radiancy divine,
    Scatter all my unbelief ;
More and more Thyself display,
Shining to the perfect day !

C. WESLEY, 1708-1788.

Hymn 59.

MELCOMBE. SAMUEL WEBBE, sen., 1740-1817.

59.

ETERNAL beam of Light Divine,
 Fountain of unexhausted love,
In Whom the Father's glories shine
 Through earth beneath, and Heaven above:

Jesu! the weary wanderer's rest!
 Give me Thy easy yoke to bear;
With stedfast patience arm my breast,
 With spotless love, and lowly fear.

Thankful I take the cup from Thee,
 Prepar'd and mingled by Thy skill:
Though bitter to the taste it be,
 Powerful the wounded soul to heal.

Be Thou, O Rock of Ages, nigh!
 So shall each murmuring thought be gone:
And grief, and fear, and care shall fly
 As clouds before the mid-day sun.

Speak to my warring passions peace:
 Say to my trembling heart, Be still:
Thy power my strength and fortress is,
 For all things serve Thy sovereign will.

O Death, where is thy sting? where now
 Thy boasted victory, O Grave?
Who shall contend with God, or who
 Can hurt whom God delights to save?

C. WESLEY, 1708-1788.

Hymn 60.

CRASSELIUS or WINCHESTER NEW.
Freylinghausen's Gesangbuch, 1704.
CRASSELIUS, 1667–1724.

60.

FORTH in Thy Name, O Lord, I go,
My daily labour to pursue ;
Thee, only Thee, resolved to know,
In all I think, or speak, or do.

The task Thy wisdom hath assigned
O let me cheerfully fulfil ;
In all my works Thy presence find,
And gladly do Thy holy will.

Thee may I set at my right hand,
Whose eyes mine inmost substance see,
And labour on at Thy command,
And offer all my works to Thee.

Give me to bear Thy easy yoke,
And every moment watch and pray ;
And still to things eternal look,
And hasten to Thy glorious day.

For Thee delightfully employ
Whate'er Thy bounteous grace hath given,
And run my course with holy joy,
And closely walk with Thee to heaven.

C. WESLEY, 1708-1788.

Hymn 61.

CHORALE.   Choralen d. der Brudergemeinen, 1784.

Hal - le - lu . . . . jah.

61.

Hark! the herald angels sing
Glory to the new-born King!
Peace on earth and mercy mild,
God and sinners reconciled!
Joyful, all ye nations, rise,
Join the triumph of the skies;
Universal nature say,
Christ, the Lord, is born to-day.

Christ, by highest heaven adored,
Christ the everlasting Lord,
Late in time behold Him come,
Offspring of a Virgin's womb.
Veiled in flesh the Godhead see;
Hail the Incarnate Deity,
Pleased as man with men to dwell,
Jesus, our Immanuel!

Hail the heavenly Prince of Peace!
Hail the Sun of Righteousness!
Light and life to all He brings,
Risen with healing in His wings.
Mild He lays His glory by,
Born that man no more may die;
Born to raise the sons of earth,
Born to give them second birth. Hallelujah.

C. Wesley, 1708-1788.

Hymn 62.

62.

JESU, Lover of my soul,
   Let me to Thy bosom fly,
While the nearer waters roll,
   While the tempest still is high!
Hide me, O my Saviour, hide,
   Till the storm of life is past;
Safe into the haven guide,
   O receive my soul at last!

Other refuge have I none;
   Hangs my helpless soul on Thee;
Leave, ah! leave me not alone,
   Still support and comfort me!
All my trust on Thee is stay'd,
   All my help from Thee I bring:
Cover my defenceless head
   With the shadow of Thy wing!

Thou, O Christ, art all I want;
   More than all in Thee I find:
Raise the fallen, cheer the faint,
   Heal the sick, and lead the blind!
Just and holy is Thy Name;
   I am all unrighteousness;
False and full of sin I am,
   Thou art full of truth and grace.

Plenteous grace with Thee is found,
   Grace to cover all my sin;
Let the healing streams abound;
   Make and keep me pure within!
Thou of Life the Fountain art,
   Freely let me take of Thee;
Spring Thou up within my heart!
   Rise to all eternity!

C. Wesley, 1708-17

Hymn 63.

BENEDICTION or
ALLELUIA DULCE CARMEN.

WEBBE's *Church Music*, 1791.
(Old Setting.)

63.

LOVE Divine, all love excelling,
    Joy of heaven, to earth come down :
Fix in us Thy humble dwelling,
    All Thy faithful mercies crown !
Jesu, Thou art all compassion,
    Pure, unbounded love Thou art ;
Visit us with Thy salvation,
    Enter every longing heart.

Come, almighty to deliver,
    Let us all Thy grace receive ;
Suddenly return, and never,
    Never more Thy temples leave.
Thee we would be always blessing,
    Serve Thee as Thy hosts above ;
Pray, and praise Thee without ceasing,
    Glory in Thy perfect love.

Finish then Thy new creation,
    Pure and spotless may we be :
Let us see Thy great salvation
    Perfectly restored by Thee :
Changed from glory into glory,
    Till in heaven we take our place,
Till we cast our crowns before Thee,
    Lost in wonder, love, and praise.

C. WESLEY, 1708-1788.

Hymn 64.

ST. WERBURGH.   SAMUEL WEBBE, sen., 1740-1816.

64.

LO! He comes! with clouds descending,
   Once for favoured sinners slain;
Thousand thousand saints attending
   Swell the triumph of His train:
      Hallelujah!
   God appears on earth to reign!

Every eye shall now behold Him,
   Robed in dreadful majesty:
They who set at nought and sold Him,
   Pierced, and nailed Him to the tree,
      Deeply wailing,
   Shall the true Messiah see.

Now Redemption, long expected,
   See in solemn pomp appear!
All His saints, by man rejected
   Rise to meet Him in the air!
      Hallelujah!
   See the Day of God appear!

Yea, Amen! let all adore Thee,
   High on Thine eternal throne!
Saviour! take Thy power and glory;
   Claim the kingdoms for Thine own!
      O come quickly!
   Thou shalt reign, and Thou alone!

C. WESLEY, 1708-1788, and M. MADAN, 1726-1790.

Hymn 65.

FRENCH or DUNDEE. Scotch Psalter, 1615.

65.

LET saints on earth in concert sing
  With those to glory gone,
For all the servants of our King,
  In earth and Heaven, are one.

One family, we dwell in Him,
  One Church, above, beneath,
Though now divided by the stream,
  The narrow stream of death.

One army of the living God,
  To His command we bow;
Part of His host have crossed the flood,
  And part are crossing now.

Ten thousand to their endless home
  This solemn moment fly;
And we are to the margin come,
  And we expect to die.

Lord Jesus, be our constant Guide,
  Then when the word is given,
Bid death's cold flood its waves divide,
  And land us safe in heaven.

C. WESLEY, 1708-1788.

Hymn 66.

BAVARIA. German Chorale.

66.

O GOD, my God, my all Thou art!
   Ere shines the dawn of rising day,
Thy sovereign light within my heart,
Thy all-enlivening power, display.

For Thee my thirsty soul doth pant,
While in this desert land I live;
And hungry as I am, and faint,
Thy love alone can comfort give.

More dear than life itself, Thy love
My heart and tongue shall still employ;
And to declare Thy praise will prove
My peace, my glory, and my joy.

In blessing Thee with grateful songs
My happy life shall glide away:
The praise that to Thy Name belongs,
Hourly, with lifted hands I'll pay.

Thy name, O God, upon my bed
Dwells on my lips, and fires my thought;
With trembling awe, in midnight shade,
I muse on all Thy hands have wrought.

In all I do I feel Thine aid;
Therefore Thy greatness will I sing,
O God, who bidst my heart be glad
Beneath the shadow of Thy wing!

C. WESLEY, 1708–1788.

Hymn 67.

ST. MICHAEL. Day's Psalter, 1565.

67.

SOLDIERS of Christ! arise,
    And put your armour on;
Strong in the strength which God supplies,
    Through His eternal Son.

Strong in the Lord of Hosts,
    And in His mighty power:
Who in the strength of Jesus trusts
    Is more than conqueror.

Stand then in His great might,
    With all His strength endued;
And take, to arm you for the fight,
    The panoply of God.

From strength to strength go on,
    Wrestle, and fight, and pray;
Tread all the powers of darkness down,
    And win the well-fought day.

That, having all things done,
    And all your conflicts past,
Ye may o'ercome, through Christ alone,
    And stand entire at last.

C. WESLEY, 1708-1788.

Hymn 68.

LEICESTER.

John Bishop, 1665-1737.
(Original Setting.)

68.

THOU hidden Source of calm repose,
  Thou all-sufficient Love Divine,
My help and refuge from my foes,
Secure I am, if Thou art mine:
And lo! from sin, and grief, and shame,
I hide me, Jesus, in Thy Name.

Thy mighty Name salvation is,
And keeps my happy soul above:
Comfort it brings, and power, and peace,
And joy, and everlasting love:
To me, with Thy dear Name, are given
Pardon, and holiness, and heaven.

Jesus, my all in all Thou art,
My rest in toil, my ease in pain;
The medicine of my broken heart;
In war, my peace; in loss, my gain:
My smile beneath the tyrant's frown;
In shame, my glory and my crown.

In want, my plentiful supply;
In weakness, my almighty power;
In bonds, my perfect liberty;
My life in Satan's darkest hour:
In grief, my joy unspeakable,
My life in death, my heaven in hell.

C. WESLEY, 1708-1788.

Hymn 69.

LEICESTER.
JOHN BISHOP, 1665–1737.
(Original Setting.)

69.

WEARY of all this wordy strife,
   These notions, forms, and modes, and names,
To Thee, the Way, the Truth, the Life,
   Whose love my simple heart inflames,
Divinely taught, at last I fly,
With Thee and Thine to live and die.

My brethren, friends, and kinsmen, these,
   Who do my Heavenly Father's will;
Who aim at perfect holiness,
   And all Thy counsels to fulfil;
Athirst to be whate'er Thou art,
And love their God with all their heart.

From these, howe'er in flesh disjoined,
   Where'er dispersed o'er earth abroad,
Unfeigned, unbounded love I find,
   And constant as the life of God;
Fountain of life, from thence it sprung,
As pure, as even, and as strong.

C. WESLEY, 1702-1788.

Hymn 70.

CHORALE.   Joh. Chr. Bach, 1643-1703.

70.

GUIDE me, O Thou Great Jehovah,
   Pilgrim through this barren land;
I am weak, but Thou art mighty,
   Hold me with Thy powerful hand;
     Bread of Heaven,
Feed me now and evermore.

Open now the crystal Fountain,
   Whence the healing streams do flow:
Let the fiery, cloudy, pillar
   Lead me all my journey through;
     Strong Deliverer,
Be Thou still my strength and shield.

When I tread the verge of Jordan,
   Bid my anxious fears subside:
Death of death, and hell's Destruction,
   Land me safe on Canaan's side;
     Songs of praises
I will ever give to Thee.

W. WILLIAMS, 1717-1791.

Hymn 71.

DUNFERMLINE. Ravenscroft's Psalter, 1621.

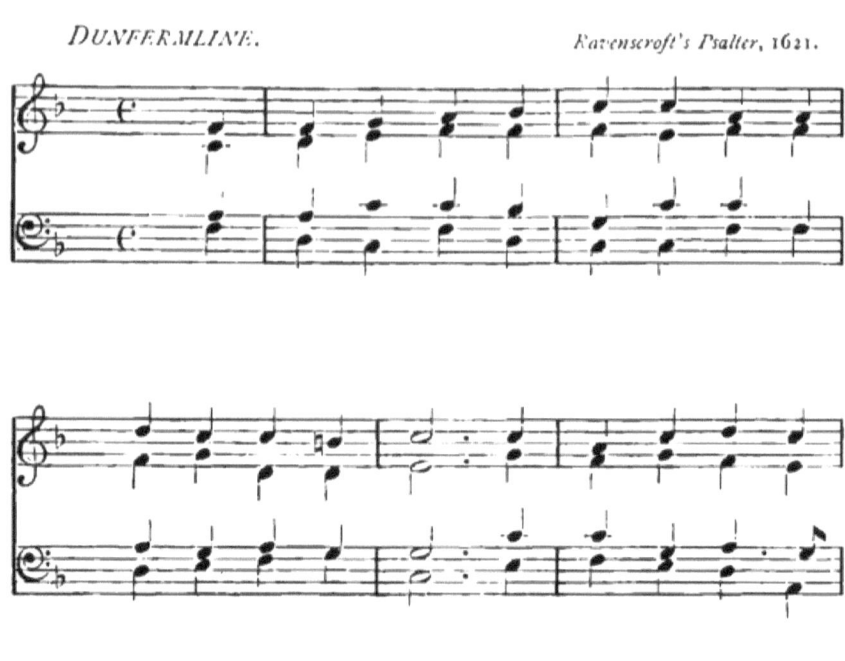

71.

Lord, while below Thy pilgrims stay,
    Our dear companion be:
Talk to us, Saviour, all the way,
    Till we come up to Thee.

Now, dearest Advocate, be nigh,
    Rejoicing every heart ;
Nor leave Thy children by and by,
    When we rise up to part.

Still bear us company, and we
    (The purchase of Thy blood)
Will bless no other Lord but Thee,
    Thou true, Thou only God.

JOHN CENNICK, 1717-1755.

Hymn 72.

WINDSOR or *DUNDEE.*   *Este's Psalter,* 1592.

72.

ETERNAL God! we look to Thee,
    To Thee for help we fly:
Thine Eye alone our wants can see,
    Thy Hand alone supply.

Lord! let Thy fear within us dwell,
    Thy love our footsteps guide :
That love will all vain love expel;
    That fear, all fear beside.

Not what we wish, but what we want,
    O let Thy grace supply :
The good unasked in mercy grant;
    The ill, though asked, deny.

J. MERRICK, 1720-1769.

Hymn 73.

NORTHAMPTON.
Dr. Croft, 1677-1727.
(Original Setting.)

73.

THY goodness, Lord, our souls confess,
   Thy goodness we adore;
A spring, whose blessings never fail,
   A sea without a shore.

Sun, moon, and stars, Thy love attest,
   In every cheerful ray;
Love draws the curtain of the night,
   And love restores the day.

Thy bounty every season crowns
   With all the bliss it yields,
With joyful clusters bend the vines,
   With harvests wave the fields.

But chiefly Thy compassions, Lord,
   Are in the Gospel seen;
There, like the sun, Thy mercy shines
   Without a cloud between.

THOMAS GIBBONS, 1720–1785.

Hymn 74.

74.

THE God of Abraham praise,
　Who reigns enthroned above:
Ancient of everlasting days,
　And God of love:
Jehovah, Great I AM,
　By earth and heaven confess'd: —
I bow and bless the sacred name
　For ever bless'd.

The God of Abraham praise,
　At whose supreme command
From earth I rise, and seek the joys
　At His right hand:
I all on earth forsake,
　Its wisdom, fame, and power;
And Him my only portion make,
　My shield and tower.

He by Himself hath sworn;
　I on His oath depend;
I shall, on eagle's wings upborne,
　To heaven ascend;
I shall behold His face,
　I shall His power adore;
And sing the wonders of His grace
　For evermore.

Though nature's strength decay,
　And earth and hell withstand,
To Canaan's bounds I urge my way,
　At His command;
The watery deep I pass,
　With Jesus in my view;
And through the howling wilderness
　My way pursue.

The God, who reigns on high,
　The great archangels sing,
And 'Holy, Holy, Holy' cry,
　'Almighty King;
Who was and is the same,
　And evermore shall be:
Jehovah, Father, Great I AM,
　We worship Thee.'

The whole triumphant host
　Give thanks to God on high;
Hail, Father, Son, and Holy Ghost,
　They ever cry;
Hail, Abraham's God and mine,
　I join the heavenly lays;
All might and majesty are Thine,
　And endless praise.

T. OLIVERS, 1725-1799.

Hymn 75.

FARRANT. RICHARD FARRANT, d. 1585.

75.

O FOR a closer walk with God,
   A calm and heavenly frame,
A light to shine upon the road
   That leads me to the Lamb!

Return, O Holy Dove! return,
   Sweet Messenger of rest;
I hate the sins that made Thee mourn,
   And drove Thee from my breast.

The dearest idol I have known,
   Whate'er that idol be,
Help me to tear it from Thy throne,
   And worship only Thee!

So shall my walk be close with God,
   Calm and serene my frame;
So purer light shall mark the road
   That leads me to the Lamb.

W. COWPER, 1731–1800.

Hymn 76.

MELCOMBE. SAMUEL WEBBE, sen., 1740-1817.

76.

JESUS, where'er Thy people meet,
  There they behold Thy mercy-seat;
Where'er they seek Thee, Thou art found,
And every place is hallowed ground.

For Thou, within no walls confined,
Inhabitest the humble mind:
Such ever bring Thee where they come,
And going take Thee to their home.

Here may we prove the power of prayer,
To strengthen faith, and sweeten care,
To teach our faint desires to rise,
And bring all heaven before our eyes.

Lord, we are few, but Thou art near:
Nor short Thine arm, nor deaf Thine ear:
O rend the heavens, come quickly down,
And make a thousand hearts Thine own.

W. COWPER, 1731–1800.

Hymn 77.

LÜBECK. *Freylinghausen's Gesangbuch,* 1704.

77.

HARK, my soul! it is the Lord;
'Tis thy Saviour, hear His word;
Jesus speaks, and speaks to thee,
'Say, poor sinner, lov'st thou Me?

'I delivered thee when bound,
And, when bleeding, healed thy wound,
Sought thee wandering, set thee right,
Turned thy darkness into light.

'Can a woman's tender care
Cease towards the child she bare?
Yes, she may forgetful be,
Yet will I remember thee.

'Mine is an unchanging love,
Higher than the heights above,
Deeper than the depths beneath,
Free and faithful, strong as death.

'Thou shalt see My glory soon,
When the work of grace is done;
Partner of My Throne shalt be;
Say, poor sinner, lov'st thou Me?'

Lord, it is my chief complaint
That my love is weak and faint;
Yet I love Thee, and adore;
O for grace to love Thee more.

W. COWPER, 1731-1800.

Hymn 78.

CHORALE.   J. NEANDER (?) 1610-1680.

78.

Rock of ages! cleft for me,
    Let me hide myself in Thee:
Let the water and the blood,
From Thy riven side which flowed,
Be of sin the double cure,
Cleanse me from its guilt and power.

Not the labours of mine hands
Can fulfil Thy law's demands;
Could my zeal no respite know,
Could my tears for ever flow,
All for sin could not atone;
Thou must save, and Thou alone.

Nothing in my hand I bring,
Simply to Thy Cross I cling;
Naked, come to Thee for dress,
Helpless, look to Thee for grace;
Foul, I to the fountain fly;
Wash me, Saviour, or I die!

While I draw this fleeting breath,
When my eye-lids close in death,
When I soar to worlds unknown,
See Thee on Thy judgment throne;
Rock of ages! cleft for me,
Let me hide myself in Thee!

A. M. Toplady, 1740—1778.

Hymn 79.

CHORALE.   J. ROSENMÜLLER, 1610-1680.

81.

O THOU unknown, Almighty Cause
  Of all my hope and fear!
In Whose dread presence, ere an hour,
  Perhaps I must appear!

If I have wander'd in those paths
  Of life I ought to shun;
As something loudly in my breast
  Remonstrates I have done;

Thou know'st that Thou hast form'ed me
  With passions wild and strong;
And list'ning to their witching voice
  Has often led me wrong.

Where human weakness has come short,
  Or frailty stept aside,
Do Thou, All-Good! for such Thou art,
  In shades of darkness hide.

Where with intention I have err'd,
  No other plea I have,
But, Thou art good; and goodness still
  Delighteth to forgive.

ROBERT BURNS, 1759-1796.

Hymn 82.

OLMÜTZ.   German.

82.

Our blest Redeemer, ere He breathed
   His tender last farewell,
A Guide, a Comforter bequeathed
   With us to dwell.

He came sweet influence to impart,
   A gracious willing Guest,
While He can find one humble heart,
   Wherein to rest.

And His that gentle Voice we hear,
   Soft as the breath of even,
That checks each thought, that calms each fear,
   And speaks of Heaven.

And every virtue we possess,
   And every conquest won,
And every thought of holiness,
   Are His alone.

Spirit of purity and grace,
   Our weakness, pitying, see:
O make our hearts Thy dwelling-place,
   And worthier Thee!

O praise the Father; praise the Son;
   Blest Spirit, praise to Thee!
All praise to God, the Three in One,
   The One in Three!

H. Auber, 1773-1862.

Hymn 83.

AUSTRIA.   J. Haydn, 1732–1809.

83.

PRAISE the Lord! ye heavens, adore Him;
    Praise Him, angels, in the height:
Sun and moon, rejoice before Him,
    Praise Him, all ye stars and light.
Praise the Lord! for He hath spoken,
    Worlds His mighty voice obeyed:
Laws which never shall be broken
    For their guidance He hath made.

Praise the Lord! for He is glorious:
    Never shall His promise fail:
God hath made His saints victorious,
    Sin and death shall not prevail.
Praise the God of our salvation;
    Hosts on high His power proclaim:
Heaven, and earth, and all creation,
    Laud and magnify His Name.

BISHOP MANT (?), 1776-1848.

Hymn 84.

84.

THOU, Whose Almighty Word
    Chaos and darkness heard,
And took their flight;
Hear us, we humbly pray;
And where the Gospel's day
Sheds not its glorious ray,
    Let there be light!

Thou Who didst come to bring
On Thy redeeming wing
    Healing and sight;
Health to the sick in mind,
Sight to the inly blind,
O now to all mankind,
    Let there be light!

Spirit of truth and love,
Life-giving, Holy Dove,
    Speed forth Thy flight!
Move on the waters' face,
Bearing the lamp of grace,
And in earth's darkest place
    Let there be light!

Holy and blessed Three,
Glorious Trinity;
    Wisdom, Love, Might,
Boundless as ocean's tide,
Rolling in fullest pride,
Through the earth, far and wide,
    Let there be light!

J. MARRIOTT, 1780—1825.

Hymn 85.

TRINITY.   W. STERNDALE BENNETT, 1816–1875.

85.

HOLY, Holy, Holy! Lord God Almighty!
Early in the morning our song shall rise to Thee;
Holy, Holy, Holy! Merciful and Mighty!
God in Three Persons, Blessèd Trinity!

Holy, Holy, Holy! all the saints adore Thee,
Casting down their golden crowns around the glassy sea;
Cherubim and Seraphim falling down before Thee,
Which wert, and art, and evermore shalt be!

Holy, Holy, Holy! though the darkness hide Thee,
Though the eye of sinful man Thy glory may not see,
Only Thou art Holy; there is none beside Thee,
Perfect in power, in love, and purity!

Holy, Holy, Holy! Lord God Almighty!
All Thy works shall praise Thy Name in earth, and sky, and sea;
Holy, Holy, Holy! Merciful and Mighty!
God in Three Persons, Blessèd Trinity!

BISHOP HEBER, 1783-1820.

Hymn 86.

THE OLD 100TH. *Day's Psalter, 1562.*

86.

THE Lord will come! the earth shall quake,
The hills their fixèd seat forsake;
And, withering, from the vault of night
The stars withdraw their feeble light.

The Lord will come! but not the same
As once in lowly form He came,
A silent Lamb to slaughter led,
The bruised, the suffering, and the dead.

The Lord will come! a dreadful form,
With wreath of flame, and robe of storm,
On cherub wings, and wings of wind,
Anointed Judge of human kind!

Can this be He Who wont to stray
A pilgrim on the world's highway;
By power oppressed, and mocked by pride?
O God! is this the Crucified?

Go, tyrants, to the rocks complain!
Go, seek the mountains cleft in vain!
But Faith, victorious o'er the tomb,
Shall sing for joy—'The Lord is come!'

BISHOP HEBER, 1783-1826.

Hymn 87.

NOTTINGHAM or *ST. MAGNUS.*   JEREMIAH CLARK, 1670-1707.

87.

THE Son of God goes forth to war,
   A kingly crown to gain,
His blood-red banner streams afar;
   Who follows in His train?

Who best can drink his cup of woe,
   Triumphant over pain,
Who patient bears his cross below,
   He follows in His train.

The Martyr first, whose eagle eye
   Could pierce beyond the grave,
Who saw his Master in the sky,
   And called on Him to save.

Like Him, with pardon on his tongue
   In midst of mortal pain,
He prayed for them that did the wrong:
   Who follows in his train?

A glorious band, the chosen few
   On whom the Spirit came,
Twelve valiant Saints, their hope they knew,
   And mocked the cross and flame.

They met the tyrant's brandished steel,
   The lion's gory mane,
They bowed their necks the death to feel;
   Who follows in their train?

A noble army, men and boys,
   The matron and the maid,
Around the Saviour's Throne rejoice
   In robes of light arrayed.

They climbed the steep ascent of heaven
   Through peril, toil, and pain;
O God, to us may grace be given
   To follow in their train.

BISHOP HEBER, 1783-1826.

Hymn 88.

HANOVER. DR. CROFT, 1677-1727.

88.

O WORSHIP the King,
  All glorious above;
O gratefully sing
  His power and His love;
Our Shield and Defender,
  The Ancient of days,
Pavilioned in splendour,
  And girded with praise.

O tell of His might,
  O sing of His grace,
Whose robe is the light,
  Whose canopy space;
His chariots of wrath
  The thunderclouds form,
And dark is His path
  On the wings of the storm.

The earth with its store
  Of wonders untold,
Almighty, Thy power
  Hath founded of old:
Hath stablished it fast
  By a changeless decree,
And round it hath cast,
  Like a mantle, the sea.

Thy bountiful care
  What tongue can recite?
It breathes in the air,
  It shines in the light;
It streams from the hills,
  It descends to the plain,
And sweetly distils
  In the dew and the rain.

  Frail children of dust,
    And feeble as frail,
  In Thee do we trust,
    Nor find Thee to fail;
  Thy mercies how tender!
    How firm to the end!
  Our Maker, Defender,
    Redeemer, and Friend!

Sir R. Grant, 1785-1838.

Hymn 89.

WOBURN. HENRY CAREY, d. 1743.

89.

WHEN gathering clouds around I view,
And days are dark, and friends are few,
On Him I lean Who not in vain
Experienced every human pain :
He sees my wants, allays my fears,
And counts and treasures up my tears.

If aught should tempt my soul to stray
From heavenly wisdom's narrow way;
To flee the good I would pursue,
Or do the sin I would not do;
Still He, Who felt temptation's power,
Shall guard me in that dangerous hour.

When vexing thoughts within me rise,
And sore dismayed my spirit dies,
Yet He, Who once vouchsafed to bear
The sickening anguish of despair,
Shall sweetly soothe, shall gently dry,
The throbbing heart, the streaming eye.

When sorrowing o'er some stone I bend
Which covers all that was a friend,
And from his hand, his voice, his smile,
Divides me for a little while;
Thou, Saviour, mark'st the tears I shed,
For Thou didst weep o'er Lazarus dead.

And O! when I have safely passed
Through every conflict but the last,
Still, Lord, unchanging, watch beside
My dying bed, for Thou hast died;
Then point to realms of cloudless day,
And wipe the latest tear away!

Sir R. Grant, 1785 1838.

Hymn 90.

90.

For the beauty of the earth,
  For the glory of the skies,
For the love which from our birth
  Over and around us lies,
    Lord of all, to Thee we raise
    This our grateful psalm of praise!

For the wonder of each hour
  Of the day and of the night,
Hill and vale, and tree and flower,
  Sun and moon, and stars of light,
    Lord of all, to Thee we raise
    This our grateful psalm of praise!

For the joy of human love,
  Brother, sister, parent, child,
Friends on earth, and friends above,
  Pleasures pure and undefiled,
    Lord of all, to Thee we raise
    This our grateful psalm of praise!

For Thy Church that evermore
  Lifteth holy hands above,
Offering up on every shore
  Her pure sacrifice of love,
    Lord of all, to Thee we raise
    This our grateful psalm of praise!

J. Pierpont, 1785-1866.

Hymn 91.

VICTORY. G. P. DA PALESTRINA, 1524-1594.

91.

JUST as I am, without one plea
   But that Thy Blood was shed for me,
And that Thou bidd'st me come to Thee,
    O Lamb of God, I come.

Just as I am, and waiting not
To rid my soul of one dark blot,
To Thee, Whose Blood can cleanse each spot,
    O Lamb of God, I come.

Just as I am, though tossed about
With many a conflict, many a doubt,
Fightings and fears within, without,
    O Lamb of God, I come.

Just as I am, poor, wretched, blind;
Sight, riches, healing of the mind,
Yea all I need, in Thee to find,
    O Lamb of God, I come.

Just as I am, Thou wilt receive,
Wilt welcome, pardon, cleanse, relieve;
Because Thy promise I believe,
    O Lamb of God, I come.

Just as I am, (Thy love unknown
Has broken every barrier down);
Now to be Thine, yea, Thine alone,
    O Lamb of God, I come.

Just as I am, of that free love
The breadth, length, depth, and height to prove,
Here for a season, then above,
    O Lamb of God, I come.

CHARLOTTE ELLIOTT, 17-3-1871

Hymn 92.

ST. BARTHOLOMEW.
HENRY DUNCALF, 1762.
(Original Setting.)

92.

LET me be with Thee where Thou art,
　　My Saviour, my Eternal Rest!
Then only will this longing heart
　Be fully and for ever blest.

Let me be with Thee where Thou art,
　Thy unveiled glory to behold!
Then only will this wandering heart
　Cease to be treacherous, faithless, cold.

Let me be with Thee where Thou art,
　Where spotless Saints Thy Name adore!
Then only will this sinful heart
　Be evil and defiled no more.

Let me be with Thee where Thou art,
　Where none can die, where none remove!
There neither death nor life will part
　Me from Thy Presence and Thy Love.

CHARLOTTE ELLIOTT, 1789-1871.

Hymn 93.

PLAYFORD.   Melody and Harmony by JOHN PLAYFORD, 1623-1693.

⁎⁎ *The last line of words to be repeated.*

93.

MY God, my Father, while I stray,
Far from my home, on life's rough way,
O teach me from my heart to say,
    'Thy will be done.'

Though dark my path, and sad my lot,
Let me be still and murmur not,
Or breathe the prayer divinely taught,
    'Thy will be done.'

What though in lonely grief I sigh
For friends beloved no longer nigh,
Submissive would I still reply,
    'Thy will be done.'

If Thou should'st call me to resign
What most I prize, it ne'er was mine;
I only yield Thee what is Thine;
    'Thy will be done.'

Let but my fainting heart be blest
With Thy sweet Spirit for its guest,
My God, to Thee I leave the rest;
    'Thy will be done.'

Renew my will from day to day,
Blend it with Thine, and take away
All that now makes it hard to say,
    'Thy will be done.'

CHARLOTTE ELLIOTT, 1789-1871.

Hymn 94.

KING'S NORTON.

JEREMIAH CLARK, 1670-1707.
Original Setting.

94.

O HELP us, Lord! each hour of need
   Thy heavenly succour give;
Help us in thought, and word, and deed,
   Each hour on earth we live!

O help us when our spirits bleed
   With contrite anguish sore;
And when our hearts are cold and dead,
   O help us, Lord, the more!

O help us, through the prayer of faith,
   More firmly to believe;
For still the more the servant hath,
   The more he shall receive.

O help us, Jesu, from on high!
   We know no help but Thee:
O help us so to live and die
   As Thine in heaven to be!

DEAN MILMAN, 1791–1868.

Hymn 95.

FRANCONIA. German, 1720.

95.

BLEST are the pure in heart,
    For they shall see our God;
The secret of the Lord is theirs;
    Their soul is Christ's abode.

The Lord, who left the heavens
    Our life and peace to bring,
To dwell in lowliness with men,
    Their Pattern and their King;

He to the lowly soul
    Doth still Himself impart;
And for His dwelling and His throne
    Chooseth the pure in heart.

Lord, we Thy presence seek;
    May ours this blessing be;
Give us a pure and lowly heart,
    A temple meet for Thee.

J. KEBLE, 1792–1866.

Hymn 96.

MELCOMBE. SAMUEL WEBBE, sen., 1740-1817.

96.

NEW every morning is the love
 Our wakening and uprising prove,
Through sleep and darkness safely brought,
Restored to life, and power, and thought.

New mercies each returning day,
Hover around us while we pray;
New perils past, new sins forgiven,
New thoughts of God, new hopes of Heaven.

If, on our daily course, our mind
Be set to hallow all we find,
New treasures still, of countless price,
God will provide for sacrifice.

We need not bid, for cloister'd cell,
Our neighbour and our work farewell,
Nor strive to wind ourselves too high
For sinful man beneath the sky:

The trivial round, the common task,
Will furnish all we ought to ask;
Room to deny ourselves; a road
To bring us daily nearer God.

Seek we no more: content with these,
Let present rapture, comfort, ease,
As Heaven shall bid them, come and go:
The secret this of rest below.

Only, O Lord, in Thy dear love
Fit us for perfect rest above;
And help us, this and every day,
To live more nearly as we pray.

J. KEBLE, 1792-1866.

Hymn 97.

ANGEL'S SONG.   ORLANDO GIBBONS, 1583-1625.

97.

Sun of my soul, Thou Saviour dear,
It is not night if Thou be near;
Oh! may no earth-born cloud arise
To hide Thee from Thy servant's eyes!

When the soft dews of kindly sleep
My wearied eyelids gently steep,
Be my last thought how sweet to rest
For ever on my Saviour's breast.

Abide with me from morn till eve,
For without Thee I cannot live;
Abide with me when night is nigh,
For without Thee I dare not die.

If some poor wandering child of Thine
Have spurned to-day the voice divine,
Now, Lord, the gracious work begin;
Let him no more lie down in sin.

Watch by the sick; enrich the poor
With blessings from Thy boundless store;
Be every mourner's sleep to-night,
Like infant's slumbers, pure and light.

Come near and bless us when we wake,
Ere through the world our way we take;
Till in the ocean of Thy love
We lose ourselves in Heaven above.

J. KEBLE, 1792–1866.

Hymn 98.

ST. FLAVIAN. Day's Psalter, 1563.

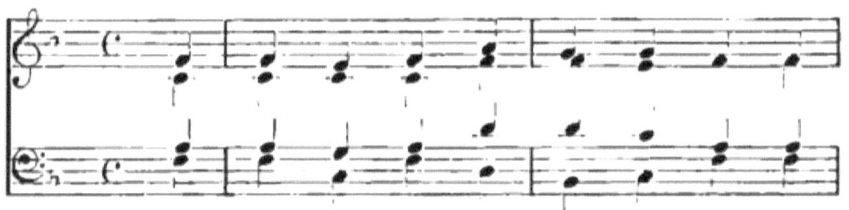

98.

THERE is a book, who runs may read,
　Which heavenly truth imparts;
And all the lore its scholars need,
　Pure eyes and Christian hearts.

The works of God above, below,
　Within us and around,
Are pages in that book to show
　How God Himself is found.

The glorious sky embracing all
　Is like the Maker's love,
Wherewith encompassed, great and small
　In peace and order move.

The moon above, the Church below,
　A wondrous race they run;
But all their radiance, all their glow,
　Each borrows of its Sun.

One Name above all glorious names
　With its ten thousand tongues
The everlasting sea proclaims,
　Echoing Angelic songs.

The raging fire, the roaring wind,
　Thy boundless power display;
But in the gentler breeze we find
　Thy Spirit's viewless way.

Two worlds are ours: 'tis only sin
　Forbids us to descry
The mystic heaven and earth within,
　Plain as the sea and sky.

Thou, Who hast given me eyes to see
　And love this sight so fair,
Give me a heart to find out Thee,
　And read Thee everywhere!

J. KEBLE, 1792-1866.

Hymn 99.

99.

WHEN God of old came down from heaven,
   In power and wrath He came;
Before His feet the clouds were riven,
   Half darkness and half flame.

But, when He came the second time,
   He came in power and love;
Softer than gale at morning prime
   Hovered His holy Dove.

The fires, that rushed on Sinai down
   In sudden torrents dread,
Now gently light, a glorious crown,
   On every sainted head.

And as on Israel's awe-struck ear
   The voice exceeding loud,
The trump, that Angels quake to hear,
   Thrilled from the deep, dark cloud;

So, when the Spirit of our God
   Came down His flock to find,
A voice from heaven was heard abroad,
   A rushing, mighty wind.

It fills the Church of God; It fills
   The sinful world around;
Only in stubborn hearts and wills
   No place for It is found.

Come Lord, come Wisdom, Love and Power,
   Open our ears to hear;
Let us not miss the accepted hour;
   Save, Lord, by love or fear.

J. Keble, 1792-1866.

Hymn 100.

OLD 121TH.
Day's Psalter, 1563.

100.

ABIDE with me; fast falls the eventide;
The darkness deepens; Lord, with me abide;
When other helpers fail, and comforts flee,
Help of the helpless, O abide with me.

Swift to its close ebbs out life's little day;
Earth's joys grow dim, its glories pass away;
Change and decay in all around I see;
O Thou Who changest not, abide with me.

I need Thy presence every passing hour;
What but Thy grace can foil the tempter's power?
Who like Thyself my guide and stay can be?
Through cloud and sunshine, Lord, abide with me.

I fear no foe with Thee at hand to bless;
Ills have no weight, and tears no bitterness;
Where is death's sting; where, grave, thy victory?
I triumph still, if Thou abide with me.

Hold Thou Thy Cross before my closing eyes;
Shine through the gloom, and point me to the skies;
Heaven's morning breaks, and earth's vain shadows flee;
In life, in death, O Lord, abide with me.

H. F. LYTE, 1793-1847.

Hymn 101.

SOUTHWELL. Denham's Psalter, 1588.

101.

FAR from my heavenly home,
    Far from my Father's breast,
Fainting I cry, 'Blest Spirit, come!
    And speed me to my rest!'

My spirit homeward turns,
    And fain would thither flee;
My heart, O Sion, droops and yearns,
    When I remember thee.

To thee, to thee, I press;
    A dark and toilsome road;
When shall I pass the wilderness,
    And reach the saints' abode?

God of my life, be near,
    On Thee my hopes I cast:
O guide me through the desert here,
    And bring me home at last!

H. F. Lyte, 1793-1847.

Hymn 102.

BENEDICTION or
ALLELUIA DULCE CARMEN.

WEBBE'S *Church Music*, 1791.
(Old Setting.)

102.

PRAISE, my soul, the King of Heaven!
    To His feet thy tribute bring:
Ransomed, healed, restored, forgiven,
    Who like thee His praise should sing?
        Hallelujah! Hallelujah!
    Praise the Everlasting King!

Praise Him for His grace and favour
    To our fathers in distress;
Praise Him still the same for ever,
    Slow to chide, and swift to bless:
        Hallelujah! Hallelujah!
    Glorious in His faithfulness!

Angels in the height, adore Him!
    Ye behold Him face to face:
Saints triumphant, bow before Him,
    Gathered in from every race!
        Hallelujah! Hallelujah!
    Praise with us the God of Grace!

H. F. LYTE, 1793-1847.

Hymn 103.

ABBEY. Scotch Psalter, 1615.

103.

O GOD, unseen yet ever near,
  Thy Presence may we feel;
And, thus inspired with holy fear,
  Before Thine Altar kneel.

Here may Thy faithful people know
  The blessings of Thy love,
The streams that through the desert flow,
  The manna from above.

We come, obedient to Thy Word,
  To feast on heavenly Food;
Our meat the Body of the Lord,
  Our drink His precious Blood.

Thus may we all Thy Word obey,
  For we, O God, are Thine;
And go rejoicing on our way,
  Renewed with strength Divine.

E. Osler, 1798–1863.

Hymn 104.

ST. JAMES.　　　　　　　　　　RAPHAEL COURTEVILLE, 1680.

104.

THOU art the Way, to Thee alone
    From sin and death we flee ;
And he who would the Father seek,
    Must seek Him, Lord, by Thee.

Thou art the Truth,—Thy word alone
    True wisdom can impart :
Thou only canst inform the mind,
    And purify the heart.

Thou art the Life,—the rending tomb
    Proclaims Thy conquering arm ;
And those who put their trust in Thee
    Nor death nor hell shall harm.

Thou art the Way, the Truth, the Life ;
    Grant us that way to know,
That truth to keep, that life to win
    Whose joys eternal flow.

BISHOP DOANE, 17 —1859.

Hymn 105.

CHORALE. Adapted from a German Chorale.

105.

LEAD, Kindly Light, amid the encircling gloom !
    Lead Thou me on !
The night is dark, and I am far from home—
    Lead Thou me on !
Keep Thou my feet ; I do not ask to see
The distant scene—one step enough for me.

I was not ever thus, nor pray'd that Thou
    Shouldst lead me on.
I loved to choose and see my path, but now
    Lead Thou me on !
I loved the garish day, and, spite of fears,
Pride ruled my will : remember not past years.

So long Thy Power hath blest me, sure it still
    Will lead me on,
O'er moor and fen, o'er crag and torrent, till
    The night is gone ;
And with the morn those angel faces smile
Which I have loved long since, and lost awhile.

                           J. H. NEWMAN, 1801–1890.

Hymn 106.

WINDSOR or DUNDEE. Este's Psalter, 1592.

106.

LORD! as to Thy dear Cross we flee,
    And plead to be forgiven,
So let Thy life our Pattern be,
    And form our souls for Heaven!

Help us, through good report and ill,
    Our daily cross to bear;
Like Thee to do our Father's Will,
    Our brethren's griefs to share.

Let grace our selfishness expel,
    Our earthliness refine,
And kindness in our bosoms dwell,
    As free and true as Thine.

If joy shall at Thy bidding fly,
    And grief's dark day come on,
We in our turn would meekly cry,
    'Father, Thy will be done!'

Kept peaceful in the midst of strife,
    Forgiving and forgiven,
O may we lead the pilgrim's life,
    And follow Thee to Heaven!

                        T. GURNEY, 1802–1862.

Hymn 107.

AUSTRIA. J. HAYDN, 1732-1809.

107.

LORD, dismiss us with Thy blessing,
　　Fill our hearts with joy and peace ;
Let us each, Thy love possessing,
　　Triumph in redeeming grace :
　　　　O refresh us,
Travelling through this wilderness !

Thanks we give and adoration
　　For Thy gospel's joyful sound ;
May the fruits of Thy salvation
　　In our hearts and lives abound :
　　　　May Thy presence
With us evermore be found !

So whene'er the signal's given
　　Us from earth to call away,
Borne on angels' wings to heaven,
　　Glad the summons to obey,
　　　　May we ever
Reign with Christ in endless day.

H. T. Buckoll, 1803-1871.

Hymn 108.

108.

'STAY, Master, stay upon this heavenly hill;
A little longer let us linger still;
With these two mighty ones of old beside,
Near to the awful Presence still abide:
Before the gates of light we trembling stand,
And touch the veil that hides the spirit-land.

'Stay, Master, stay! we breathe a purer air;
This life is not the life that waits us there;
Thoughts, feelings, flashes, glimpses, come and go;
We cannot speak them—nay, we do not know:
Wrapt in this cloud of light, we seem to be
The thing we fain would grow—eternally.'

'No!' saith the Lord, 'the hour is past; we go:
Our home, our life, our duties lie below.
While here we kneel upon the mount of prayer
The plough lies waiting in the furrow there:
Here we sought God that we might know His will,
There we must do it—serve Him—seek Him still.

'If man aspires to reach the throne of God,
O'er the dull plains of earth must lie the road;
He who best does his lowly duty there,
Shall mount the highest in a nobler sphere:
At God's own feet our spirits seek their rest,
And he is nearest Him who serves Him best.'

S. GREG, 1804-1877.

Hymn 109.

OLD 117TH.
Old French Psalter, 1562.

109.

LORD of the harvest, once again
We thank Thee for the ripened grain;
For crops safe carried, sent to cheer
Thy servants through another year;
For all sweet holy thoughts supplied
By seed-time, and by harvest-tide.

The bare dead grain, in autumn sown,
Its robe of vernal green puts on;
Glad from its wintry grave it springs,
Fresh garnished by the King of Kings :
So, Lord, to those who sleep in Thee
Shall new and glorious bodies be.

Nor vainly of Thy Word we ask
A lesson from the reaper's task :
So shall Thine Angels issue forth;
The tares be burnt; the just of earth,
To wind and storm exposed no more,
Be gathered to their Father's store.

Daily, O Lord, our prayers be said,
As Thou hast taught, for daily bread :
But not alone our bodies feed,
Supply our fainting spirits' need :
O Bread of life, from day to day,
Be Thou their Comfort, Food, and Stay.

JOSEPH ANSTICE, 1808-1836.

Hymn 110.

OLD 137TH.   Day's Psalter, 1563.

110.

I HEARD the voice of Jesus say,
 'Come unto Me and rest;
Lay down, thou weary one, lay down
 Thy head upon My Breast:'

I came to Jesus as I was,
 Weary, and worn, and sad;
I found in Him a resting-place,
 And He has made me glad.

I heard the voice of Jesus say,
 'Behold, I freely give
The living water, thirsty one,
 Stoop down, and drink, and live:'

I came to Jesus, and I drank
 Of that life-giving stream;
My thirst was quenched, my soul revived,
 And now I live in Him.

I heard the voice of Jesus say,
 'I am this dark world's Light;
Look unto Me, thy morn shall rise,
 And all thy day be bright:'

I looked to Jesus and I found
 In Him my Star, my Sun;
And in that Light of life I'll walk
 Till travelling days are done.

HORATIUS BONAR, 1805-1889.

Hymn 111.

OBERSTEIN.   German.

111.

O EVERLASTING Light,
  Giver of dawn and day,
Dispeller of the ancient night
  In which creation lay :

O everlasting Health,
  From which all healing springs,
Our Bliss, our Treasure, and our Wealth,
  To Thee our spirit clings !

O everlasting Truth,
  Truest of all that's true ;
Sure Guide of erring age and youth,
  Lead us, and teach us too !

O everlasting Strength,
  Uphold us in the way ;
Bring us, in spite of foes, at length
  To joy, and light, and day !

O everlasting Love,
  Wellspring of grace and peace ;
Pour down Thy fulness from above,
  Bid doubt and trouble cease !

HORATIUS BONAR, 1808-1889.

Hymn 112.

SIGILLUS. Michael Siegel, 1648.

112.

Thy way, not mine, O Lord,
  However dark it be!
Lead me by Thine own hand,
  Choose out the path for me.

Smooth let it be or rough,
  It will be still the best;
Winding or straight, it leads
  Right onward to Thy rest.

I dare not choose my lot;
  I would not, if I might;
Choose Thou for me, my God;
  So shall I walk aright.

The kingdom that I seek
  Is Thine; so let the way
That leads to it be Thine;
  Else I must surely stray.

Take Thou my cup, and it
  With joy or sorrow fill,
As best to Thee may seem;
  Choose Thou my good and ill:

Choose Thou for me my friends,
  My sickness or my health;
Choose Thou my cares for me,
  My poverty or wealth.

Not mine, not mine the choice,
  In things or great or small;
Be Thou my guide, my strength,
  My wisdom and my all!

Horatius Bonar, 1808–1889

Hymn 113.

UFFINGHAM. Jeremiah Clark, 1670-1707.

113.

O LORD of Hosts! Almighty King!
Behold the sacrifice we bring!
To every arm Thy strength impart;
Thy Spirit shed through every heart!

Wake in our breasts the living fires,
The holy faith, that warmed our sires!
Thy hand hath made our Nation free;
To die for her is serving Thee.

Be Thou a Pillared Flame to show
The midnight snare, the silent foe;
And, when the battle thunders loud,
Still guide us in its moving Cloud!

God of all Nations! Sovereign Lord!
In Thy dread Name we draw the sword;
We lift the meteor-flag on high
That fills with light our troubled sky.

From Treason's rent, from Murder's stain,
Guard Thou its folds till peace shall reign;
Till fort and field, till shore and sea,
Join our loud anthem, Praise to Thee!

O. W. Holmes, *b.* 1809.

Hymn 114.

ARCADELT.
JACQUES ARCADELT, 1540.

114.

JERUSALEM, the holy!
Jerusalem the blest!
From highest heaven descending
In bridal beauty drest;
Bride of the Lamb! thy glory,
The light of God alone,
Shines through thee clear as crystal,
And like a jasper stone.

Within thee is no temple,
No holy house of prayer;
For the Lord God Almighty
And the Lamb thy temple are:
No need of sun to lighten,
No need of moon to shine;
Thy sunshine is God's glory,
The Lamb thy Light divine.

Jerusalem, the holy!
My spirit longs to be
Within thy walls of jasper,
Thy gates of pearl to see;
And through the sunless city
To walk thy streets of gold,
And in thy moonless beauty
God's glory to behold.

Give me, O Lord, the patience
To labour and endure;
Grant that these eyes may see Thee,
Give me a heart that's pure:
Write Thine own Name upon it,
That, after earth's long strife,
My name may be found written
In the Lamb's book of Life!

J. S. B. Monsell, 1811-1875.

Hymn 115.

115.

LORD! to Thy Holy temple
  Return, return again!
Come back, and fill with glory
  The hearts and ways of men!
Not as a lowly Infant,
  Unnoticed and unknown,
But in the royal splendour
  Of Thine Eternal throne!

O Thou, Whom we delight in,
  The Messenger of love,
Come to Thy temple quickly
  Back from Thy throne above!
But who may bide Thy coming,
  Who hear Thy footsteps tread,
Who stand when Thou appearest,
  Thou Judge of quick and dead?

Thy Spirit send before Thee,
  Till every heart, restored
By His new life, adore Thee,
  Their only God and Lord!
And make our offerings pleasant
  As in the days of old,
And as in former happy years
  Of which our fathers told!

Come back! and fill Thy temple,
  Built up of human hearts,
With that abiding Presence
  Which never more departs!
Come! where the prostrate nations
  Before Thy feet shall fall;
Come! with Thy holy Angels,
  Come back the Lord of all!

J. S. B. MONSELL, 1811–1875.

Hymn 116.

OLD 25TH PSALM. Day's Psalter, 1563.

116.

THOU art gone up on high
   To mansions in the skies,
And round Thy throne unceasingly
   The songs of praise arise.
But we are lingering here,
   With sin and care opprest;
Lord, send Thy promised Comforter,
   And lead us to Thy rest.

Thou art gone up on high:
   But Thou didst first come down,
Through earth's most bitter misery
   To pass unto Thy crown:
And girt with griefs and fears
   Our onward course must be;
But only let that path of tears
   Lead us at last to Thee.

Thou art gone up on high:
   But Thou shalt come again
With all the bright ones of the sky
   Attendant in Thy train.
O by Thy saving power
   So make us live and die,
That we may stand, in that dread hour,
   At Thy right hand on high!

Emma Toke, 1812-1878.

Hymn 117.

ARUNDEL. S. WEBBE, sen., 1740-1817.

(234)

117.

WE thank Thee, Lord, for this fair earth,
   The glittering sky, the silver sea,
For all their beauty, all their worth,
   Their light and glory, come from Thee.

Thanks for the flowers that clothe the ground,
   The trees that wave their arms above,
The hills that gird our dwellings round,
   As Thou dost gird Thine own with love.

Yet teach us still how far more fair,
   More glorious, Father, in Thy sight,
Is one pure deed, one holy prayer,
   One heart that holds Thy Spirit's might.

So while we gaze, with thoughtful eye,
   On all the gifts Thy love has given,
Help us in Thee to live and die,
   By Thee to rise from earth to Heaven.

Bishop Cotton, 1813-1866.

Hymn 118.

CHORALE.   J. S. BACH, 1685-1750.

118.

PART I.

HE is gone: beyond the skies
A cloud receives Him from our eyes:
Gone beyond the highest height
Of mortal gaze or angels' flight;
Through the veils of time and space,
Passed into the Holiest Place;
All the toil, the sorrow done,
All the battle fought and won.

He is gone: and we remain,
In this world of sin and pain;
In the void which He has left
On this earth, of Him bereft,
We have still His work to do,
We can still His path pursue:
Seek Him both in friend and foe,
In ourselves His image show.

He is gone: we heard Him say,
'Good that I should go away.'
Gone is that dear form and face,
But not gone His present grace;
Though Himself no more we see,
Comfortless we cannot be;
No! His Spirit still is ours,
Quickening, freshening, all our powers.

PART II.

He is gone: towards their goal
World and Church must onward roll;
Far behind we leave the past;
Forwards are our glances cast:
Still His words before us range
Through the ages as they change:
Wheresoe'er the truth shall lead,
He will give whate'er we need.

He is gone: but we once more
Shall behold Him as before;
In the Heaven of heavens the same,
As on earth He went and came.
In the many mansions there,
Place for us He will prepare:
In that world unseen, unknown,
He and we may yet be one.

He is gone: but not in vain;
Wait until He comes again:
He is risen, He is not here,
Far above this earthly sphere:
Evermore in heart and mind,
There our peace in Him we find;
To our own Eternal Friend,
Thitherward let us ascend.

A. P. STANLEY, 1815-1881.

Hymn 119.

CHORALE. J. S. Bach (?), 1685-1750.

120.

PSALM XXIII.

THE King of Love my Shepherd is,
    Whose goodness faileth never ;
I nothing lack if I am His
    And He is mine for ever.

Where streams of living water flow
    My ransomed soul He leadeth,
And, where the verdant pastures grow,
    With food celestial feedeth.

Perverse and foolish oft I strayed,
    But yet in love He sought me,
And on His shoulder gently laid,
    And home, rejoicing, brought me.

In death's dark vale I fear no ill
    With Thee, dear Lord! beside me ;
Thy rod and staff my comfort still,
    Thy Cross before to guide me.

Thou spread'st a Table in my sight,
    Thy Unction grace bestoweth ;
And O! what transport of delight
    From Thy pure Chalice floweth!

And so through all the length of days
    Thy goodness faileth never ;
Good Shepherd! may I sing Thy praise
    Within Thy House for ever!

            SIR HENRY BAKER, 1821-1877.

Hymn 121.

COLESHILL.   Scotch Psalter, 1635.

121.

O GOD of Truth! Whose living Word
    Upholds whate'er has breath,
Look down on Thy created sons
    Enslaved by sin and death.

Set up Thy standard, Lord! that we,
    Who claim a Heavenly birth,
May march with Thee to smite the lies
    That vex Thy groaning earth.

And would we join that blest array,
    And follow in the might
Of Him, the Faithful and the True,
    In raiment clean and white?

How can we fight for Truth and God,
    Enthralled to lies and sin?
He who would wage such war on earth
    Must first be true within.

O God of Truth! for Whom we long,
    O Thou that hearest prayer,
Do Thine own battle in our hearts,
    And slay the falsehood there.

So, tried in Thy refining fire,
    From every lie set free,
In us Thy perfect Truth shall dwell,
    And we may fight for Thee.

T. HUGHES, 1823-1889.

Hymn 122.

ANGELUS.   JOHANN SCHEFFLER, 1624-1677.

(244)

122.

AT even, ere the sun was set,
The sick, O Lord, around Thee lay;
O in what divers pains they met!
O with what joy they went away!

Once more 'tis eventide, and we,
Oppress'd with various ills, draw near:
What if Thy form we cannot see?
We know and feel that Thou art here.

O Saviour Christ, our woes dispel;
For some are sick, and some are sad,
And some have never loved Thee well,
And some have lost the love they had;

And some have found the world is vain,
Yet from the world they break not free;
And some have friends who give them pain,
Yet have not sought a friend in Thee.

And none, O Lord, have perfect rest,
For none are wholly free from sin;
And they, who fain would serve Thee best,
Are conscious most of wrong within.

O Saviour Christ, Thou too art man;
Thou hast been troubled, tempted, tried;
Thy kind but searching glance can scan
The very wounds that shame would hide.

Thy touch has still its ancient power;
No word from Thee can fruitless fall;
Hear in this solemn evening hour,
And in Thy mercy heal us all.

H. TWELLS, b. 1823.

Hymn 123.

ST. MATTHEW. DR. CROFT, 1677-1727.

123.

THE shadows of the evening hours
    Fall from the darkening sky ;
Upon the fragrance of the flowers
    The dews of evening lie :
Before Thy throne, O Lord of Heaven,
    We kneel at close of day ;
Look on Thy children from on high
    And hear us while we pray.

The sorrows of Thy servants, Lord,
    O do not Thou despise,
But let the incense of our prayers
    Before Thy mercy rise :
The brightness of the coming night
    Upon the darkness rolls ;
With hopes of future glory chase
    The shadows on our souls.

Slowly the rays of daylight fade ;
    So fade within our heart
The hopes in earthly love and joy,
    That one by one depart :
Slowly the bright stars, one by one,
    Within the heavens shine ;
Give us, O Lord, fresh hopes in Heaven,
    And trust in things divine.

Let peace, O Lord, Thy peace, O God,
    Upon our souls descend ;
From midnight fears and perils, Thou
    Our trembling hearts defend :
Give us a respite from our toil,
    Calm and subdue our woes ;
Through the long day we labour, Lord,
    O give us now repose.

ADELAIDE ANNE PROCTER, 1825-1864.

Hymn 124.

124.

ETERNAL Father! strong to save,
Whose arm doth bind the restless wave,
Who bidd'st the mighty ocean deep,
Its own appointed limits keep:
Oh, hear us when we cry to Thee
For those in peril on the sea.

O Saviour! Whose almighty Word
The winds and waves submissive heard,
Who walkedst on the foaming deep
And calm amid its rage didst sleep:
Oh, hear us when we cry to Thee
For those in peril on the sea.

O Sacred Spirit! Who didst brood
Upon the chaos dark and rude,
Who bad'st its angry tumult cease,
And gavest light, and life, and peace:
Oh, hear us when we cry to Thee
For those in peril on the sea.

O Trinity of love and power,
Our brethren shield in danger's hour;
From rock and tempest, fire and foe,
Protect them wheresoe'er they go;
And ever let there rise to Thee
Glad hymns of praise from land and sea.

W. WHITING, 1825–1878.

Hymn 125.

CHORALE. JOH. RUD. AHLE, 1625-1673.

125.

NOW the labourer's task is o'er;
   Now the battle day is past;
Now upon the farther shore
   Lands the voyager at last.
Father, in Thy gracious keeping
Leave we now Thy servant sleeping.

There the tears of earth are dried;
   There its hidden things are clear;
There the work of life is tried
   By a juster Judge than here.
Father, in Thy gracious keeping
Leave we now Thy servant sleeping.

There the sinful souls, that turn
   To the Cross their dying eyes,
All the love of Christ shall learn
   At His Feet in Paradise.
Father, in Thy gracious keeping
Leave we now Thy servant sleeping.

There no more the powers of hell
   Can prevail to mar their peace;
Christ the Lord shall guard them well,
   He who died for their release.
Father, in Thy gracious keeping
Leave we now Thy servant sleeping.

'Earth to earth, and dust to dust,'
   Calmly now the words we say,
Leaving *him* to sleep in trust
   Till the Resurrection-day.
Father, in Thy gracious keeping
Leave we now Thy servant sleeping.

J. ELLERTON.

Hymn 126.

ST. LUKE. H. PURCELL, 1658-1695.

126.

JOB iii, 17–20.

HOW still and peaceful is the grave!
    Where, life's vain tumults past,
Th' appointed house, by Heav'n's decree,
    Receives us all at last.

The wicked there from troubling cease,
    Their passions rage no more;
And there the weary pilgrim rests
    From all the toils he bore.

There rest the pris'ners, now releas'd
    From slav'ry's sad abode;
No more they hear th' oppressor's voice,
    Or dread the tyrant's rod.

There servants, masters, small and great,
    Partake the same repose;
And there, in peace, the ashes mix
    Of those who once were foes.

All, levell'd by the hand of Death,
    Lie sleeping in the tomb;
Till God in judgment calls them forth,
    To meet their final doom.

From the Scotch Paraphrases.

Hymn 127.

ST. MATTHIAS. ORLANDO GIBBONS, 1583-1625.

127.

REVELATION xxi. 1–9.

LO! what a glorious sight appears
   To our admiring eyes!
The former seas have pass'd away,
   The former earth and skies.

From heav'n the new Jerus'lem comes,
   All worthy of its Lord;
See all things now at last renew'd,
   And paradise restor'd!

The God of glory down to men
   Removes His bless'd abode;
He dwells with men; His people they,
   And He His people's God.

His gracious hand shall wipe the tears
   From ev'ry weeping eye:
And pains and groans, and griefs and fears,
   And death itself, shall die.

Behold, I change all human things!
   Saith He, whose words are true;
Lo! what was old is pass'd away,
   And all things are made new!

I am the First, and I the Last,
   Through endless years the same;
I AM, is My memorial still,
   And My eternal Name.

From the Scotch Paraphrases.

Hymn 128.

BANGOR. Ravenscroft's Psalter, 1621.

128.

PROVERBS viii. 22–36.

KEEP silence, all ye sons of men,
  And hear with rev'rence due;
Eternal Wisdom from above
  Thus lifts her voice to you:

I was th' Almighty's chief delight
  From everlasting days,
Ere yet His arm was stretched forth
  The heav'ns and earth to raise.

Before the sea began to flow,
  And leave the solid land,
Before the hills and mountains rose,
  I dwelt at His right hand.

When first He rear'd the arch of heav'n,
  And spread the clouds on air,
When first the fountains of the deep
  He open'd, I was there.

There I was with Him, when He stretch'd
  His compass o'er the deep,
And charg'd the ocean's swelling waves
  Within their bounds to keep.

With joy I saw th' abode prepar'd
  Which men were soon to fill:
Them from the first of days I lov'd,
  Unchang'd, I love them still.

Now therefore hearken to my words,
  Ye children, and be wise:
Happy the man that keeps my ways;
  The man that shuns them dies.

Where dubious paths perplex the mind,
  Direction I afford;
Life shall be his that follows me,
  And favour from the Lord.

From the Scotch Paraphrases.

Hymn 129.

CHORALE. J. G. Schicht, 1753-1823.

129.

THE Lord ascendeth up on high,
The Lord hath triumphed gloriously,
  In power and might excelling!
The grave and hell are captive led,
Lo! He returns, our glorious Head,
  To His eternal dwelling!

The Heavens with joy receive their Lord,
By Saints, by Angel hosts adored;
  O Day of exultation!
O earth! adore thy glorious King,
His Rising, His Ascension sing,
  With grateful adoration!

Our great High Priest hath gone before,
Now on His Church His grace to pour,
  And still His love He giveth:
O may our hearts to Him ascend,
May all within us upward tend
  To Him who ever liveth!

Author unknown.

Hymn 130.

EASTER HYMN. *Lyra Davidica*, 1708.

130.

JESUS Christ is risen to-day,
　　　　　　Alleluia!
Our triumphant holy day,
　　　　　　Alleluia!
Who did once upon the Cross,
　　　　　　Alleluia!
Suffer to redeem our loss.
　　　　　　Alleluia!

Hymns of praise then let us sing,
　　　　　　Alleluia!
Unto Christ, our heavenly King,
　　　　　　Alleluia!
Who endured the Cross and grave,
　　　　　　Alleluia!
Sinners to redeem and save.
　　　　　　Alleluia!

But the pain which He endured
　　　　　　Alleluia!
Our salvation hath procured;
　　　　　　Alleluia!
Now above the sky He's King,
　　　　　　Alleluia!
Where the Angels ever sing.
　　　　　　Alleluia!

　　　　　　　　Author unknown.

Hymn 131.

CHORALE. HANS LEO HASSLER, 1564-1612.

131.

O SACRED Head, surrounded
  By crown of piercing thorn !
O bleeding Head, so wounded,
  Reviled, and put to scorn !
Death's pallid hue comes o'er Thee,
  The glow of life decays,
Yet Angel-hosts adore Thee,
  And tremble as they gaze.

I see Thy strength and vigour
  All fading in the strife,
And death with cruel rigour
  Bereaving Thee of life ;
O agony and dying !
  O love to sinners free !
Jesu, all grace supplying,
  O turn Thy Face on me.

In this Thy bitter Passion,
  Good Shepherd, think of me
With Thy most sweet compassion,
  Unworthy though I be :
Beneath Thy Cross abiding
  For ever would I rest,
In Thy dear love confiding,
  And with Thy presence blest.

St. BERNARD of Clairvaux, 1091-1153.
Translated by Sir H. BAKER, 1821-1877.

Hymn 132.

WEIMAR.   MELCHIOR VULPIUS, 1560–1616.

132.

BRIEF life is here our portion;
   Brief sorrow, short-lived care;
The life that knows no ending,
   The tearless life, is there.

O happy retribution!
   Short toil, eternal rest;
For mortals and for sinners
   A mansion with the blest!

And now we fight the battle,
   But then shall wear the crown
Of full and everlasting
   And passionless renown;

And now we watch and struggle,
   And now we live in hope,
And Sion in her anguish
   With Babylon must cope;

But He, Whom now we trust in,
   Shall then be seen and known;
And they that know and see Him
   Shall have Him for their own.

The morning shall awaken,
   The shadows shall decay,
And each true-hearted servant
   Shall shine as doth the day.

There God, our King and Portion,
   In fulness of His grace,
Shall we behold for ever,
   And worship face to face.

O sweet and blessèd country,
   The home of God's elect!
O sweet and blessèd country
   That eager hearts expect!

Jesu, in mercy bring us
   To that dear land of rest;
Who art, with God the Father
   And Spirit, ever blest.

BERNARD, of Cluny, c. 1150.
Translated by J. M. NEALE, 1818-1866.

Hymn 133.

CHORALE (MUNICH).   Attributed to J. HERMANN, 1620.

133.

For thee, O dear, dear Country!
    Mine eyes their vigils keep;
For very love, beholding
    Thy happy Name, they weep:
O one, O only mansion,
    O Paradise of joy!
Where tears are ever banished,
    And smiles have no alloy!

With jasper glow thy bulwarks,
    Thy streets with emeralds blaze;
The sardius and the topaz
    Unite in thee their rays:
Thy ageless walls are bonded
    With amethyst unpriced;
The Saints build up its fabric,
    The Corner-stone is Christ!

Thou hast no shore, fair ocean!
    Thou hast no time, bright day!
Dear fountain of refreshment
    To pilgrims far away!
Jesu, in mercy bring us
    To that dear land of rest;
Who art, with God the Father,
    And Spirit, ever blest!

Bernard, of Cluny, c. 1150.
Translated by J. M. Neale, 1818–1866.

Hymn 134.

VICTORY.

G. P. DA PALESTRINA, 1524-1594.

134.

THE strife is o'er, the battle done;
Now is the Victor's triumph won;
O let the song of praise be sung.
     Alleluia!

Death's mightiest powers have done their worst,
And Jesus hath His foes dispersed;
Let shouts of praise and joy outburst.
     Alleluia!

On the third morn He rose again
Glorious in majesty to reign;
O let us swell the joyful strain,
     Alleluia!

Lord, by the stripes which wounded Thee
From death's dread sting Thy servants free,
That we may live, and sing to Thee
     Alleluia!

From Latin Hymn of 12th Century.
Translated by F. POTT, *b.* 1832.

Hymn 135.

CHORALE. Arranged from German Chorale, 'Wir Christenleut' from *Dresdener Gesangbuch*, 1594.

135.

THE sun is sinking fast,
  The daylight dies;
Let love awake, and pay
  Her evening sacrifice.

As Christ upon the Cross
  His head inclined,
And to His Father's hands
  His parting soul resigned;

So now herself my soul
  Would wholly give
Into His sacred charge,
  In Whom all spirits live:

So now beneath His eye
  Would calmly rest,
Without a wish or thought
  Abiding in the breast;

Save that His will be done,
  Whate'er betide;
Dead to herself, and dead
  In Him to all beside.

Thus would I live; yet now
  Not I, but He
In all His power and love
  Henceforth alive in me.

One sacred Trinity!
  One Lord Divine!
May I be ever His,
  And He for ever mine!

From Latin Hymn.
Translated by E. Caswall, 1814-1878.

Hymn 136.

BABYLON.   T. CAMPION, d. 1619.

136.

THAT day of wrath, that dreadful day,
When heaven and earth shall pass away,
What power shall be the sinner's stay?
How shall he meet that dreadful day?

When, shrivelling like a parched scroll,
The flaming heavens together roll;
When louder yet, and yet more dread,
Swells the high trump that wakes the dead.

O! on that day, that wrathful day,
When man to judgment wakes from clay,
Be Thou, O Christ, the sinner's stay,
Though heaven and earth shall pass away.

THOMAS OF CELANO, c. 1208-1275.
Translated by SIR WALTER SCOTT, 1771-1832.

Hymn 137.

CHORALE. MARTIN LUTHER, 1483-1546.

137.

A SAFE Stronghold our God is still,
    A trusty Shield and Weapon;
He'll help us clear from all the ill
    That in our days shall happen.
The ancient Prince of Hell
Hath risen with purpose fell;
Strong mail of craft and power
He weareth in this hour;
On earth is not his fellow.

With force of arms we nothing can,
    Full soon we were down-ridden;
But for us fights the proper Man,
    Whom God Himself hath bidden.
Ask ye, Who is this same?
Christ Jesus is His Name,
The Lord Zebaoth's Son;
He, and no other one,
Shall conquer in the battle.

And were this world all Devils o'er,
    And watching to devour us,
We lay it not to heart so sore;
    Not they can overpower us.
And let the Prince of Ill
Look grim as e'er he will,
He harms us not a whit:
For why? His doom is writ;
A word shall quickly slay him.

God's Word, for all their craft and force,
    One moment will not linger,
But, spite of Hell, shall have its course;
    'Tis written by His finger.
And though they take our life,
Goods, honour, children, wife,
Yet is their profit small;
These things shall vanish all,
The City of God remaineth!

MARTIN LUTHER, 1483-1546.
Translated by THOMAS CARLYLE, 1795-1881.

Hymn 138.

138.

OUT of the depths I cry to Thee,
　　Lord, hear me, I implore Thee!
Bend down Thy gracious ear to me,
　　Let my prayer come before Thee!
If Thou rememb'rest each misdeed,
If each should have its rightful meed,
　　Who may abide Thy presence?

Our pardon is Thy gift, Thy love
　　And grace alone avail us;
Our works could ne'er our guilt remove,
　　The strictest life must fail us:
That none may boast himself of aught,
But own in fear Thy grace hath wrought
　　What in him seemeth righteous.

And thus my hope is in the Lord,
　　And not in mine own merit;
I rest upon His faithful word
　　To them of contrite spirit;
That He is merciful and just—
Here is my comfort and my trust,
　　His help I wait with patience.

Though great our sins, and sore our woes,
　　His grace much more aboundeth;
His helping love no limit knows,
　　Our utmost need it soundeth:
Our kind and faithful Shepherd, He
Who shall at last set Israel free
　　From all their sin and sorrow.

MARTIN LUTHER, 1483-1546.
Translated by C. WINKWORTH, 1829-1878.

Hymn 139.

SPIERS. MARTIN LUTHER, 1483-1546.

139.

Do I not love Thee, Lord most High,
  In answer to Thy love for me?
I seek no other liberty
But that of being bound to Thee.

May memory no thought suggest
But shall to Thy pure glory tend;
My understanding find no rest
Except in Thee, its only end.

My God, I here protest to Thee,
No other will I have than Thine;
Whatever Thou hast given me
I here again to Thee resign.

All mine is Thine; say but the word,
Whate'er Thou willest,—be it done:
I know Thy love, all-gracious Lord;
I know it seeks my good alone.

Apart from Thee all things are nought:
Then grant, O my supremest bliss!
Grant me to love Thee as I ought:—
Thou givest all in giving this!

Ignatius Loyola, 1491-1556.
Translated by E. Caswall, 1814-1878.

Hymn 140.

CHORALE.
MARTIN LUTHER, 1483-1546.

140.

GREAT God, what do I see and hear!
 The end of things created!
The Judge of mankind doth appear,
 On clouds of glory seated!
The trumpet sounds, the graves restore
The dead, which they contained before:
 Prepare, my soul, to meet Him!

The dead in Christ shall first arise,
 At the last trumpet sounding;
Caught up to meet Him in the skies,
 With joy their Lord surrounding:
No gloomy fears their souls dismay,
His presence sheds eternal day
 On those prepared to meet Him!

But sinners, filled with guilty fears,
 Behold His wrath prevailing;
For they shall rise, and find their tears
 And sighs are unavailing:
The day of grace is past and gone;
Trembling, they stand before the throne
 All unprepared to meet Him!

Great God, what do I see and hear!
 The end of things created!
The Judge of mankind doth appear,
 On clouds of glory seated!
Low at His Cross I view the day,
When heaven and earth shall pass away,
 And thus prepare to meet Him!

1st verse by B. Ringwaldt, 1530-1598.
W. B. Collyer, 1782-1854.

Hymn 141.

CHORALE.   ?PH. NICOLAI, 1556–1608.

141.

'Wake! Wake! Wake!' The watch are crying;
 From tower to tower the word is flying;
  'Arise, Jerusalem, arise!'
Midnight's gloom our eyes confoundeth;
But hark, how clear their call resoundeth!
  'Where are ye, O ye virgins wise?
  Up, see your lamps are bright!
  The Bridegroom is in sight.
   Hallelujah.
  Away, away, in glad array,
  Go, meet Him; 'tis His wedding-day!'

Zion hears; no more she sleepeth;
She hastes to rise; her glad heart leapeth;
 The word is sure; her Friend is nigh.
Lo! He comes in heaven's splendour,
Most strong in truth, in grace most tender;
 Her light grows clear, her star climbs high.
  So come, God's crownèd Son,
  Who hast the vict'ry won.
   Come, Lord Jesus.
  We long to see the day when we
  Shall hold the feast of love with Thee.

Unto Thee be glory given
By all on earth and all in heaven;
 Bid harp and cymbal swell the strain.
So they sing, the choirs immortal;
And we shall pass the pearly portal,
 And we shall stand among Thy train.
  No eye hath ever seen,
  No ear hath ever heard
   Such great gladness.
  We will therefore to Thee outpour
  Loud Hallelujahs evermore.

Ph. Nicolai, 1556-1608.
Translated by E. J. Palmer.

Hymn 142.

142.

THE morning star upon us gleams.
How full of grace and truth His beams,
　　How passing fair His splendour!
Good Shepherd, David's proper heir,
My King in heav'n, Thou dost me bear
　　Upon Thy bosom tender.
　　　　Nearest,
　　　　Dearest,
　　　Highest, brightest,
　　　Thou delightest
　　　Still to love me,
Thou, so high enthroned above me.

Strike deep into this heart of mine
Thy rays of love, Thou star divine,
　　And fire its dying embers:
And grant that nought have power to part
Me from Thy Body, Lord, Who art
　　The life of all Thy members.
　　　　I stand
　　　　Thy hand
　　　Ever taking,
　　　Ne'er forsaking:
　　　Nought shall ail me;
Bread of life, Thou wilt not fail me.

O holy Jesus, when the light
Of Thy dear face shines on me bright,
　　Then heav'nly joy doth thrill me.
O Lord, my sure and stedfast good,
Thy Word, Thy Spirit, Body, Blood,—
　　With life, new life, they fill me.
　　　　This day,
　　　　I pray,
　　　Mercy showing,
　　　Grace bestowing,
　　　Look on me, Lord,
Thy own word is all my plea, Lord.

Thou, mighty Father, in Thy Son
Didst love me, ere Thou hadst begun
　　This ancient world's foundation.
Thy Son hath made a friend of me,
And when in spirit Him I see
　　I've done with tribulation.
　　　　What bliss
　　　　Is this!
　　　Where He liveth,
　　　Me He giveth
　　　Life for ever;
Nought from His love can me sever.

　　Lift up the voice and strike the string,
　　Let all glad sounds of music ring
　　　　In God's high praises blended.
　　Christ will be with me all the way,
　　To-day, to-morrow, every day,
　　　　Till travelling days be ended.
　　　　　　Sing out,
　　　　　　Ring out,
　　　　　Triumph glorious
　　　　　O victorious
　　　　　Chosen nation;
　　Praise the God of your salvation.

Ph. Nicolai, 1556-1608.
From the version in the Wurtemberger Gesangbuch.
Translated by E. J. Palmer.

Hymn 143.

143.

IN Thee is gladness
Amid all sadness,
Jesus, Sunshine of my heart!
By Thee are given
The gifts of Heaven;
Thou the true Redeemer art!
Our souls Thou wakest,
Our bonds Thou breakest;
Who trusts Thee surely
Hath built securely,
He stands for ever: Hallelujah!
Our hearts are pining
To see Thy shining,
Dying or living
To Thee are cleaving,
Nought can us sever: Hallelujah!

If He is ours
We fear no powers,
Nor of earth, nor sin, nor death;
He sees and blesses
The worst distresses,
He can change them with a breath!
Wherefore the story
Tell of His glory
With heart and voices;
All heaven rejoices
In Him for ever: Hallelujah!
We shout for gladness,
Triumph o'er sadness,
Love Thee and praise Thee,
And still shall raise Thee
Glad hymns for ever: Hallelujah!

T. LINDEMANN, 1580–1630.
Translated by C. WINKWORTH, 1829–1878.

Hymn 144.

CHORALE. J. CRÜGER, 1598-1662.

(288)

144.

NOW all give thanks to God,
    Heart, voice, and hand in chorus.
Let all the world confess,
    ' The Lord doth great things for us.'
He from our mother's womb
    And tott'ring babyhood
Hath kept us to this hour,
    And done us endless good.

God give us all through life
    Peace that no trouble shaketh;
God fill our hearts with joy
    That no man from us taketh;
In every time of need
    Be with us, strong to save;
And keep us in His grace
    Here and beyond the grave.

All glory, honour, praise
    To Him who made and feeds us,
To Him Who saved, to Him
    Who into all truth leads us,
One God, the Lord most High;
    As it hath ever been,
Is now, shall ever be,
    World without end. Amen.

                      MARTIN RINCKART, 1586-1649.
                      Translated by F. J. PALMER.

Hymn 145.

CHORALE. MELCHIOR FRANK, 1580-1639.

145.

JERUSALEM, thou city fair and high,
  Would God I were in thee!
  My longing heart fain, fain to thee would fly.
It will not stay with me;
Far over vale and mountain,
Far over field and plain,
It hastes to seek its Fountain
And quit this world of pain.

Oh happy day, and yet far happier hour,
When wilt thou come at last?
When fearless to my Father's love and power,
Whose promise standeth fast,
My soul I gladly render,
For surely will His hand
Lead her with guidance tender
To heaven her fatherland.

And when within that lovely Paradise,
At last I safely dwell
From out my soul what songs of bliss shall rise,
What joy my lips shall tell,
While holy saints are singing
Hosannas o'er and o'er,
Pure Hallelujahs ringing
Around me evermore.

J. M. MEYFART, 1590–1642.
Translated by C. WINKWORTH, 1829–1878.

Hymn 146.

CHORALE. J. G. Ebeling, 1620-1672.

146.

All my heart this night rejoices,
      As I hear,
      Far and near,
Sweetest angel voices :
'Christ is born !' their choirs are singing,
      Till the air
      Everywhere
Now with joy is ringing !

Hark ! a Voice from yonder manger,
      Soft and sweet,
      Doth entreat,
' Flee from woe and danger ;
Brethren, come ! from all doth grieve you
      You are freed ;
      All you need
I will surely give you !'

Come, then, let us hasten yonder ;
      Here let all,
      Great and small,
Kneel in awe and wonder ;
Love Him Who with love is yearning :
      Hail the star
      That from afar
Bright with hope is burning !

                    P. GERHARDT, 1606-1676.
             Translated by C. WINKWORTH, 1829-1878.

Hymn 147.

ST. BRIDE.

Dr. S. Howard, 1710-1782.
(Original Setting.)

147.

Commit thou all thy griefs
   And ways into His hands,
To His sure truth and tender care,
   Who earth and heaven commands.

Who points the clouds their course,
   Whom winds and seas obey:
He shall direct thy wandering feet,
   He shall prepare thy way.

Thou on the Lord rely,
   So safe shalt thou go on;
Fix on His work thy steadfast eye,
   So shall thy work be done.

No profit canst thou gain
   By self-consuming care;
To Him commend thy cause, His ear
   Attends the softest prayer.

Thy everlasting truth,
   Father, Thy boundless love,
Sees all Thy children's wants, and knows
   What best for each will prove.

Thou everywhere hast sway,
   And all things serve thy might;
Thy every act pure blessing is,
   Thy path unsullied light.

When Thou arisest, Lord,
   What shall thy work withstand?
Whate'er Thy children want, thou giv'st;
   And who shall stay Thy hand?

P. Gerhardt, 1606-1676.
Translated by J. Wesley, 1703-1791.

Hymn 148.

CHORALE. German, 1539.

148.

NOW woods are all reposing,
Beasts, men, their eyes are closing,
   The whole world sinks to sleep.
But ye, my powers, up, wake you,
Sleep must not yet o'ertake you;
   Ye have a watch with God to keep.

Sun, where hast thou retreated?
Thy foe hath thee defeated,
   The night hath thee foredone.
Without is night victorious,
But in my soul shines glorious
   My Jesus, my unconquered Sun.

Now all around is darkling,
But golden stars are sparkling
   From out the deep blue sky.
So shall I rise in gladness
From out this vale of sadness,
   And shine before my God on high.

My eyes now all unwilling
Their watches are fulfilling;
   Soon sleep will seal them quite.
But Thou, who Israel keepest,
Thou slumb'rest not, nor sleepest;
   Be Thou my eye, my watch to-night.

A covert, Jesus, make me
Beneath Thy wings, and take me
   To sleep upon Thy breast.
If Satan rage to tear me,
Bid angels comfort bear me,
   And sing, 'This child unharmed shall rest.'

Fret not ye, my beloved,
Your feet shall not be moved,
   The Lord your souls shall keep.
Bright angels shall attend you,
And all night long defend you;
   So gives He His beloved sleep.

P. GERHARDT, 1606-1676.
Translated by E. J. PALMER.

Hymn 149.

150.

PRAISE thou the Lord, O my soul; let thy song upward soaring
Join with the songs of the angels in heaven adoring.
    Brethren, rejoice;
  Wake the lute, lift up the voice,
Loudly His praises out-pouring.

Praise thou the Lord, the all-glorious King of creation;
He hath on eagles' wings borne thee through all tribulation.
    Give Him thy heart;
  He it is Who doth impart
Joy to thee, life and salvation.

Praise thou the Lord, Who with marvellous wisdom hath made thee,
Decked thee with health, and with loving hand guided and stayed thee.
    How oft in grief
  Hath not He brought thee relief,
Spreading His wings for to shade thee.

Praise thou the Lord; look and see how thy life He sustaineth;
Think of the rivers of love that from heaven He raineth.
    God from above
  Stoopeth to give thee His love :
His mighty arm who restraineth?

Praise thou the Lord, O my soul; all that in me is, praise Him.
Bless thou His name with His people here gathered to praise Him.
    He is thy light;
  Keep Him for aye in thy sight.
Praise Him, for evermore praise Him.

                          J. NEANDER, 1610-1680.
                         Translated by E. J. PALMER.

Hymn 151.

CHORALE. J. H. SCHEIN, 1586-1630.

151.

O LOVE, Who formedst me to wear
  The image of Thy Godhead here;
Who soughtest me with tender care
  Through all my wanderings wild and drear;
O Love, I give myself to Thee,
Thine ever, only Thine to be.

O Love, Who ere life's earliest dawn
  On me Thy choice hast gently laid;
O Love, Who here as man wast born,
  And like to us in all things made;
O Love, I give myself to Thee,
Thine ever, only Thine to be.

O Love, Who once in time was slain,
  Pierced through and through with bitter woe;
O Love, Who, wrestling thus, didst gain
  That we eternal joy might know:
O Love, I give myself to Thee,
Thine ever, only Thine to be.

O Love, Who lovest me for aye,
  Who for my soul dost ever plead;
O Love, Who didst my ransom pay,
  Whose power sufficeth in my stead;
O Love, I give myself to Thee,
Thine ever, only Thine to be.

O Love, Who once shalt bid me rise
  From out this dying life of ours;
O Love, Who once above yon skies,
  Shalt set me in the fadeless bowers:
O Love, I give myself to Thee,
Thine ever, only Thine to be.

J. SCHEFFLER, 1624–1677.
Translated by C. WINKWORTH, 1829–1878.

Hymn 152.

CHORALE. J. ROSENMÜLLER, 1610–1680.

152.

NOT in anger, mighty God,
  Not in anger smite us;
We must perish if Thy rod
  Justly should requite us:
    We are nought;
    Sin hath brought,
Lord, Thy wrath upon us;
Yet have mercy on us!

Show me now a Father's love,
  And His tender patience;
Heal my wounded soul, remove
  These too sore temptations:
    I am weak;
    Father, speak
Thou of peace and gladness;
Comfort Thou my sadness!

Father, hymns to Thee we raise,
  Here and once in Heaven;
And the Son and Spirit praise,
  Who our bonds have riven:
    Evermore
    We adore
Thee, Whose grace hath stirred us,
And Whose pity heard us!

J. G. ALBINUS, 1624–1679.
Translated by C. WINKWORTH, 1827–1878.

Hymn 153.

CHORALE or PSALM 38. C. GOUDIMEL, 1510-1572.

153.

Come, my soul, thou must be waking;
    Now is breaking
O'er the earth another day:
    Come, to Him Who made this splendour
        See thou render
All thy feeble strength can pay.

Gladly hail the light returning;
    Ready burning
Be the incense of thy powers:
    For the night is safely ended;
        God hath tended
With His care thy helpless hours.

Pray that He may prosper ever
    Each endeavour,
When thine aim is good and true;
    But that He may ever thwart thee,
        And convert thee,
When thou evil wouldst pursue.

Think that He thy ways beholdeth;
    He unfoldeth
Every fault that lurks within;
    Every stain of shame glossed over
        Can discover,
And discern each deed of sin.

Fettered to the fleeting hours,
    All our powers
Vain and brief are borne away:
    Time, my soul, thy ship is steering,
        Onward veering,
To the gulf of death a prey.

Mayst thou then on life's last morrow,
    Free from sorrow,
Pass away in slumber sweet:
    And released from death's dark sadness,
        Rise in gladness,
That far brighter Sun to greet.

Only God's free gifts abuse not,
    Light refuse not,
But His Spirit's voice obey;
    Soon shall joy thy brow be wreathing
        Splendour breathing
Fairer than the fairest day.

                Baron von Canitz, 1654-1699.
                Translated by H. J. Buckoll, 1803-1871.

Hymn 154.

CHORALE.   J. NEANDER, 1610-1680.

154.

WHO are these like stars appearing,
   These, before God's throne who stand?
Each a golden crown is wearing,
  Who are all this glorious band?
    Hallelujah! hark they sing,
    Praising loud their heavenly King.

Who are these of dazzling brightness,
  These in God's own truth arrayed,
Clad in robes of purest whiteness,
  Robes whose lustre ne'er shall fade,
    Ne'er be touched by Time's rude hand?
    Whence come all this glorious band?

These are they who have contended
  For their Saviour's honour long,
Wrestling on till life was ended,
  Following not the sinful throng:
    These, who well the fight sustained,
    Triumph by the Lamb have gained.

These are they whose hearts were riven,
  Sore with woe and anguish tried,
Who in prayer full oft have striven
  With the God they glorified;
    Now, their painful conflict o'er,
    God has bid them weep no more.

These, the Almighty contemplating,
  Did as priests before Him stand,
Soul and body always waiting
  Day and night at His command;
    Now in God's most holy place
    Blest they stand before His face.

               H. T. SCHENK, 1656-1727.
               Translated by F. E. COX.

155.

O RISEN Lord! O conqu'ring King!
  O Life of all the living!
To-day that peace of Easter bring
Which comes but of Thy giving!
Once Death, our foe,
Had laid Thee low,
Now hast Thou rent his bonds in twain,
Now art Thou risen Who once wast slain!

Oh that to know Thy victory
To us were inly granted,
And these cold hearts might catch from Thee
The glow of faith undaunted;
Thy quenchless light,
Thy glorious might
Still comfortless and lonely leave
The soul that cannot yet believe.

Then break through our hard hearts Thy way,
O Jesus, Lord of glory!
Kindle the lamp of faith to-day,
Teach us to sing before Thee
For joy at length,
That in Thy strength
We too may rise whom sin had slain,
And Thine eternal rest attain.

And when our tears for sin o'erflow,
Do Thou in love draw near us,
Thy precious gift of peace bestow,
Let Thy bright presence cheer us,
That so may we,
O Christ, from Thee
Drink in the life that cannot die,
And keep true Easter feasts on high.

J. H. BÖHMER, 1674-1749.
Translated by C. WINKWORTH, 1829-1878.

Hymn 156.

CRASSELIUS or WINCHESTER NEW. *Freylinghausen's Gesangbuch*, 1704.
CRASSELIUS, 1667-1724.

156.

On Jordan's bank the Baptist's cry
Announces that the Lord is nigh;
Awake, and hearken, for He brings
Glad tidings of the King of kings.

Then cleansed be every breast from sin;
Make straight the way for God within;
Prepare we in our hearts a home,
Where such a mighty Guest may come.

For Thou art our salvation, Lord,
Our Refuge, and our great Reward;
Without Thy grace we waste away,
Like flowers that wither and decay.

To heal the sick stretch out Thine Hand,
And bid the fallen sinner stand;
Shine forth, and let Thy light restore
Earth's own true loveliness once more.

All praise, Eternal Son, to Thee
Whose Advent doth Thy people free
Whom with the Father we adore
And Holy Ghost for evermore.

C. Coffin, 1676–1749.
Translated by T. Chandler, 1806–1876.

Hymn 157.

NORFOLK. DR. S. HOWARD, 1710-1782.

157.

What star is this, with beams so bright,
More beauteous than the noonday light?
It shines to herald forth the King,
And Gentiles to His cradle bring.

See now fulfilled what God decreed,
'From Jacob shall a star proceed';
And eastern sages with amaze
Upon the wondrous vision gaze.

The guiding star above is bright:
Within them shines a clearer light,
Which leads them on with power benign
To seek the Giver of the sign.

True love can brook no dull delay;
Nor toil nor dangers stop their way:
Home, kindred, father-land and all
They leave at their Creator's call.

O Jesu, while the star of grace
Allures us now to seek Thy Face,
Let not our slothful hearts refuse
The guidance of that light to use.

All glory, Jesu, be to Thee
For this Thy glad Epiphany,
Whom with the Father we adore
And Holy Ghost for evermore.

C. COFFIN, 1676–1749.
Translated by T. CHANDLER, 1806–1876.

Hymn 158.

ELY.   Dr. T. Turton, 1780–1864.

158.

O THOU to Whose all-searching sight
The darkness shineth as the light,
Search, prove my heart: it pants for Thee;
O burst these bonds, and set it free!

If in this darksome wild I stray,
Be Thou my Light, be Thou my Way:
No foes, no violence I fear,
No fraud, while Thou, my God, art near.

When rising floods my soul o'erflow,
When sinks my heart in waves of woe,
Jesu, Thy timely aid impart,
And raise my head, and cheer my heart.

Saviour, where'er Thy steps I see,
Dauntless, untired, I follow Thee:
O let Thy hand support me still,
And lead me to Thy holy hill!

If rough and thorny be the way,
My strength proportion to my day;
Till toil, and grief, and pain shall cease,
Where all is calm, and joy, and peace.

G. TERSTEEGEN, 1697-1769.
Translated by J. WESLEY, 1703-1791.

Hymn 159.

Edited by H. KUGELMANN, 1540.
Harmonized by MENDELSSOHN.

CHORALE.

159.

THOU hidden Love of God, Whose height,
   Whose depth unfathomed, no man knows;
I see from far Thy beauteous light,
   Inly I sigh for Thy repose:
My heart is pained, nor can it be
At rest, till it finds rest in Thee.

Is there a thing beneath the sun
   That strives with Thee my heart to share?
O tear it thence, and reign alone,
   The Lord of every motion there!
Then shall my heart from earth be free,
When it has found repose in Thee.

O Love! Thy sovereign aid impart,
   To save me from forbidden care;
Chase this self-will through all my heart,
   Through all its latent mazes there;
Make me Thy duteous child, that I
Ceaseless may 'Abba, Father,' cry.

Each moment draw from earth away
   My heart, that lowly waits Thy call;
Speak to mine inmost soul, and say,
   I am thy Life, thy God, thy All!
To feel Thy power, to hear Thy voice,
To taste Thy love, be all my choice!

G. TERSTEEGEN, 1697-1769.
Translated by J. WESLEY, 1703-1791.

Hymn 160.

CHORALE. J. CRÜGER, 1598-1662.

160.

JESUS lives! no longer now
   Can thy terrors, Death, appal us;
Jesus lives! by this we know
   Thou, O Grave, canst not enthral us.
              Hallelujah!

Jesus lives! henceforth is death
   Entrance-gate of life immortal;
This shall calm our trembling breath,
   When we pass its gloomy portal.
              Hallelujah!

Jesus lives! for us He died;
   Then, alone to Jesus living,
Pure in heart may we abide,
   Praise to Him and glory giving.
              Hallelujah!

Jesus lives! our hearts know well,
   Nought from us His love shall sever;
Life, nor death, nor powers of hell
   Part us now from Christ for ever.
              Hallelujah!

Jesus lives! to Him the throne
   High o'er heaven and earth is given;
May we go where He is gone,
   Live and reign with Him in heaven.
              Hallelujah!

                    C. F. GELLERT, 1715-1769.
                    Translated by F. E. Cox.

Hymn 161.

161.

O LORD, Thy heavenly grace impart,
And fix my frail inconstant heart:
Henceforth my chief desire shall be
To dedicate myself to Thee,
  To Thee, my God, to Thee!

Whate'er pursuits my time employ,
One thought shall fill my soul with joy:
That silent, secret thought shall be,
That all my hopes are fixed on Thee,
  On Thee, my God, on Thee!

Thy glorious eye pervadeth space,
Thou'rt present, Lord, in every place;
And, wheresoe'er my lot may be,
Still shall my spirit cleave to Thee,
  To Thee, my God, to Thee!

Renouncing every worldly thing,
Safe 'neath the covert of Thy wing,
My sweetest thought henceforth shall be,
That all I want I find in Thee,
  In Thee, my God, in Thee!

J. F. OBERLIN, 1740-1826.
Translated by Mrs. D. WILSON.

Hymn 162.

CLEWER. German.

162.

O LET him, whose sorrow
   No relief can find,
Trust in God, and borrow
   Ease for heart and mind.

Where the mourner weeping
   Sheds the secret tear,
God His watch is keeping,
   Though none else be near.

God will never leave thee,
   All thy wants He knows,
Feels the pains that grieve thee,
   Sees thy cares and woes.

Raise thine eyes to heaven
   When thy spirits quail,
When, by tempests driven,
   Heart and courage fail.

When in grief we languish,
   He will dry the tear,
Who His children's anguish
   Soothes with succour near.

All our woe and sadness,
   In this world below,
Balance not the gladness
   We in heaven shall know.

Jesu, Holy Saviour,
   In the realms above
Crown us with Thy favour,
   Fill us with Thy love.

H. S. Oswald, 1751-1834.
Translated by F. E. Cox.

163.

JAM lucis orto sidere
　　Deum precemur supplices,
Ut in diurnis actibus
Nos servet a nocentibus.

Linguam refraenans temperet,
Ne litis horror insonet;
Visum fovendo contegat,
Ne vanitates hauriat.

Sint pura cordis intima,
Absistat et vecordia;
Carnis terat superbiam
Potus cibique parcitas:

Ut cum dies abscesserit,
Noctemque sors reduxerit,
Mundi per abstinentiam
Ipsi canamus gloriam.

Deo Patri sit gloria,
Ejusque soli Filio,
Cum Spiritu Paraclito,
Nunc et per omne saeculum.

St. Ambrose, 340-397.

164.

ALES diei nuntius
Lucem propinquam praecinit;
Nos excitator mentium
Jam Christus ad vitam vocat.

'Auferte,' clamat, 'lectulos
Ægros, soporos, desides;
Castique, recti, sobrii
Vigilate; jam sum proximus.'

Jesum ciamus vocibus
Flentes, precantes, sobrii:
Intenta supplicatio
Dormire cor mundum vetat.

Tu, Christe, somnum disjice,
Tu rumpe noctis vincula;
Tu solve peccatum vetus,
Novumque lumen ingere.

Deo Patri sit gloria
Ejusque soli Filio,
Sancto simul cum Spiritu
Nunc et per omne saeculum.

AURELIUS CLEMENS PRUDENTIUS, 348-413.

165.

Nox et tenebrae et nubila
Confusa mundi et turbida,—
Lux intrat, albescit polus,
Christus venit,— discedite.

Caligo terrae scinditur,
Percussa solis spiculo,
Rebusque jam color redit
Vultu nitentis sideris.

Te, Christe, solum novimus,
Te mente pura et simplici
Flendo et canendo quaesumus:
Intende nostris sensibus.

Sunt multa fucis illita
Quae luce purgentur tua:
Tu, Rex, Eoi sideris
Vultu sereno illumina.

Deo Patri sit gloria,
Ejusque soli Filio,
Cum Spiritu Paraclito,
Nunc et per omne saeculum.

Aurelius Clemens Prudentius, 348–413.

Hymn 169.

Hymn 170.

170.

LAUDA, Sion, Salvatorem,
Lauda Ducem et Pastorem
    In hymnis et canticis;
Quantum potes, tantum aude,
Quia major omni laude,
    Nec laudare sufficis.

Laudis thema specialis,
Panis vivus et vitalis
    Hodie proponitur,
Quem in sacrae mensa coenae
Turbae fratrum duodenae
    Datum non ambigitur.

Bone Pastor, Panis vere,
Jesu, nostri miserere;
Tu nos pasce, nos tuere,
Tu nos bona fac videre
    In terra viventium:
Tu, qui cuncta scis et vales,
Qui nos pascis hic mortales,
Tuos ibi commensales,
Cohaeredes et sodales
    Fac sanctorum civium.

        St. Thomas Aquinas, 1224–1274.

INDEX OF FIRST LINES.

A.

	HYMN
A safe Stronghold our God is still	137
Abide with me; fast falls the eventide	100
Ales diei nuntius	164
All my heart this night rejoices	146
All people that on earth do dwell	5
All praise to Him Who dwells in bliss	56
As pants the hart for cooling streams	42
At even, ere the sun was set	122
Awake, my soul, and with the sun	22

B.

Before Jehovah's awful throne	27
Behold the sun, that seem'd but now	7
Blest are the pure in heart	95
Blest be Thy Love, dear Lord	15
Brief life is here our portion	132

C.

Christ, Whose glory fills the skies	58
Christians, awake, salute the happy morn	33
Come, gracious Spirit, heavenly Dove	31
Come, Holy Ghost, our souls inspire	11
Come, my soul, thou must be waking	153
Come, O come, in pious lays	8
Come, O Thou Traveller unknown	57
Commit thou all thy griefs	147

D.

	HYMN
Dies irae, dies illa	169
Do I not love Thee, Lord most High	139

E.

Eternal beam of Light Divine	59
Eternal Father! strong to save	124
Eternal God, of beings First	32
Eternal God! we look to Thee	72

F.

Far from my heavenly home	101
For ever and for ever, Lord	49
For the beauty of the earth	90
For thee, O dear, dear Country!	133
Forth in Thy Name, O Lord, I go	60
From lowest depths of woe	48

G.

Glory to Thee, my God, this night	23
Great God, what do I see and hear!	140
Guide me, O Thou great Jehovah	70

H.

Hark, my soul, how everything	16
Hark, my soul! it is the Lord	77
Hark, the glad sound!	52
Hark! the herald angels sing	61

INDEX.

	HYMN
He is gone: beyond the skies	118
He that has God his Guardian made	46
Help us, O Lord! behold we enter	149
Holy, Holy, Holy! Lord God Almighty!	85
How are Thy servants blest, O Lord	34
How still and peaceful is the grave	126

I.

I heard the voice of Jesus say	110
I lift my heart to Thee	4
In Thee is gladness	143
In the time of my distress	9

J.

Jam lucis orto sidere	163
Jerusalem on high	21
Jerusalem, the holy!	114
Jerusalem, thou city fair and high	145
Jesu dulcis memoria	168
Jesu, Lover of my soul	62
Jesus Christ is risen to-day	130
Jesus lives! no longer now	160
Jesus! Thy boundless love to me	54
Jesus, where'er Thy people meet	76
Just as I am, without one plea	91

K.

Keep silence, all ye sons of men	128

L.

Lauda, Sion, Salvatorem	170
Lead, Kindly Light	105
Let all the just to God with joy	40
Let me be with Thee where Thou art	92
Let saints on earth in concert sing	65
Let us with a gladsome mind	13
Lo! God is here! let us adore	55
Lo! He comes! with clouds descending	64
Lo! what a glorious sight appears	127

	HYMN
Lord! as to Thy dear Cross we flee	106
Lord, dismiss us with Thy blessing	107
Lord of the harvest, once again	109
Lord of the worlds above	25
Lord, to Thy holy Temple	115
Lord, while below Thy pilgrims stay	71
Love Divine, all love excelling	63

M.

Maker of the human heart	119
My God, and is Thy Table spread	53
My God, my Father, while I stray	93
My Shepherd is the living Lord	3
My soul, repeat His praise	30

N.

New every morning is the love	96
Not in anger, mighty God	152
Now all give thanks to God	144
Now it belongs not to my care	17
Now the labourer's task is o'er	125
Now woods are all reposing	148
Nox et tenebrae et nubila	165

O.

O Everlasting Light	111
O for a closer walk with God	75
O God of Hosts, the mighty Lord	45
O God of Truth! Whose living word	121
O God, our help in ages past	26
O God, my God, my all Thou art!	66
O God, my heart is fix'd, 'tis bent	43
O God, my strength and fortitude	2
O God, unseen yet ever near	103
O help us, Lord! each hour of need	94
O let him, whose sorrow	162
O Lord of Hosts! Almighty King!	113
O Lord, Thy heavenly grace impart	161
O Lord, turn not Thy face from me	6
O Love, Who formedst me to wear	151
O risen Lord! O conqu'ring King!	155

INDEX.

	HYMN
O Sacred Head, surrounded	131
O Thou, the first, the greatest Friend	80
O Thou, to Whom all creatures bow	39
O Thou to Whose all-searching sight	158
O Thou unknown, Almighty Cause	81
O worship the King	88
On Jordan's bank the Baptist's cry	156
Our blest Redeemer, ere He breathed	82
Out of the depths I cry to Thee	138

P.

Praise, my soul, the King of Heaven	102
Praise the Lord! ye heavens adore Him	83
Praise thou the Lord, O my soul; let thy song upward soaring	150

R.

Ring out, ye crystal spheres	14
Rock of ages! cleft for me	78

S.

Soldiers of Christ! arise	67
Stay, Master, stay upon this heavenly hill	108
Sun of my soul, Thou Saviour dear	97

T.

That day of wrath, that dreadful day	136
The eternal gates lift up their heads	19
The God of Abraham praise	74
The God of Love my Shepherd is	10
The King of Love my Shepherd is	120
The Lord ascendeth up on high	129
The Lord my pasture shall prepare	35
The Lord will come! the earth shall quake	86
The morning star upon us gleams	142
The seas are quiet when the winds give o'er	12
The shadow of the evening hours	123

	HYMN
The Son of God goes forth to war	87
The spacious firmament on high	36
The strife is o'er, the battle done	134
The sun is sinking fast	135
There is a book, who runs may read	98
There is a land of pure delight	28
Thou art gone up on high	116
Thou art the Way—to Thee alone	104
Thou hidden Love of God, Whose height	159
Thou hidden Source of calm repose	68
Thou, Lord, by strictest search hast known	50
Thou, Whom chiefest I desire	79
Thou, Whose Almighty Word	84
Through all the changing scenes of life	41
Thy goodness, Lord, our souls confess	73
Thy way, not mine, O Lord	112
To bless Thy chosen race	44

U.

Up to those bright and gladsome hills	20

V.

Veni, Creator Spiritus	166
Veni, Sancte Spiritus	167

W.

'Wake! Wake! Wake!' the watch are crying	141
Weary of all this wordy strife	69
We thank Thee, Lord, for this fair earth	117
What star is this, with beams so bright	157
When all Thy mercies, O my God	37
When gathering clouds around I view	89
When God of old came down from Heaven	99
When I survey the wondrous Cross	29
When rising from the bed of death	38

(337) B b

INDEX.

	HYMN		HYMN
While shepherds watched their flocks by night	24	**Y.** Ye boundless realms of joy .	51
Who are these like stars appearing .	154	Ye holy angels bright . . .	18
With glory clad, with strength arrayed	47	Ye that have spent the silent night	1

www.ingramcontent.com/pod-product-compliance
Lightning Source LLC
Chambersburg PA
CBHW030307240426
43673CB00040B/1093